ALABASTER
GUIDED MEDITATIONS

LUKE

READ | REFLECT | RESPOND | REST

Guided Meditations by Jan Johnson

NLT

An imprint of InterVarsity Press
Downers Grove, Illinois

InterVarsity Press
P.O. Box 1400, Downers Grove, IL 60515-1426
ivpress.com | email@ivpress.com

InterVarsity Press® is the book-publishing division of InterVarsity Christian
Fellowship/USA®, a movement of students and faculty active on campus at
hundreds of universities, colleges, and schools of nursing in the United States
of America, and a member movement of the International Fellowship of
Evangelical Students. For information about local and regional activities, visit
intervarsity.org.

ISBN 978-0-8308-4725-9 (print)

Printed in the United States of America ∞

InterVarsity Press is committed to ecological stewardship and to the conservation
of natural resources in all our operations. This book was printed using
sustainably sourced paper.

Library of Congress Cataloging-in-Publication Data
  A catalog record for this book is available from the Library of Congress.

P   13   12   11   10   9   8   7   6   5   4   3   2   1
Y   31   30   29   28   27   26   25   24   23   22   21

INTRODUCING ALABASTER GUIDED MEDITATIONS

In these pages you'll find an evocative pairing of photographs with the New Living Translation of the Bible. To deepen your experience of both Scripture and image, we've added guided meditations, written by experienced Bible teachers.

Lectio divina is a practice of Scripture reading, prayer, and meditation with a long and rich heritage in the Christian tradition. As early as the fourth century, the term *lectio divina* was being used by Christians like St. Ambrose, St. Hilary of Poitiers, and St. Augustine to refer to reading Scripture. The practice was developed over the years and formalized in the twelfth century—notably by St. John of the Cross, whose famous maxim says, "Seek in reading and you will find in meditation; knock in prayer and it will be opened to you in contemplation." These are the four traditional steps of lectio divina: reading, meditation, prayer, and contemplation. These steps are presented here as (1) Read, (2) Reflect, (3) Respond, and (4) Rest.

Lectio divina invites us into the Bible's world, prompting us to imagine the biblical scene, to feel what the writers of Scripture might have felt, and to listen for what the Holy Spirit might be prompting us to consider. Visio divina applies this process to images, inviting us into prayerful interaction with visual works of art. Both lectio divina and visio divina can be practiced individually or in group settings.

The Alabaster Guided Meditations combine lectio divina with visio divina, inviting us to contemplate the words of Scripture by way of the photographs that accompany the text. Readers can focus on the words of Scripture alone or add in the visual element, using the fourfold lectio divina pattern.

These meditations invite us to enter into Holy Scripture in a new way—not as a passive text to be studied, but as the living Word of God, spoken anew to us.

CREDITS

Author of Guided Meditations
Jan Johnson

Creative Director
Bryan Ye-Chung

Business Director
Brian Chung

Operations Director
Willa Jin

Product Designer
Tyler Zak

Special Thanks
Josephine Law

Photographers
Jacob Chung
Ian Teraoka
Bryan Ye-Chung

Models
GianCarlo Aguilar
Aaron Ashby
Calvin Boyd
Nick Kwok
Joshua Kwok
Mark Mekailian
Chris Miller
Clay Song
Jessica Ticas

1

INTRODUCTION

¹ Many people have set out to write accounts about the events that have been fulfilled among us. ² They used the eyewitness reports circulating among us from the early disciples. ³ Having carefully investigated everything from the beginning, I also have decided to write an accurate account for you, most honorable Theophilus, ⁴ so you can be certain of the truth of everything you were taught.

THE BIRTH OF JOHN THE BAPTIST FORETOLD

⁵ When Herod was king of Judea, there was a Jewish priest named Zechariah. He was a member of the priestly order of Abijah, and his wife, Elizabeth, was also from the priestly line of Aaron. ⁶ Zechariah and Elizabeth were righteous in God's eyes, careful to obey all of the Lord's commandments and regulations. ⁷ They had no children because Elizabeth was unable to conceive, and they were both very old. ⁸ One day Zechariah was serving God in the Temple, for his order was on duty that week. ⁹ As was the custom of the priests, he was chosen by lot to enter the sanctuary of the Lord and burn incense. ¹⁰ While the incense was being burned, a great crowd stood outside, praying. ¹¹ While Zechariah was in the sanctuary, an angel of the Lord appeared to him, standing to the right of the incense altar. ¹² Zechariah was shaken and overwhelmed with fear when he saw him. ¹³ But the angel said, "Don't be afraid, Zechariah! God has heard your prayer. Your wife, Elizabeth, will give you a son, and you are to name him John. ¹⁴ You will have great joy and gladness, and many will rejoice at his birth, ¹⁵ for he will be great in the eyes of the Lord. He must never touch wine or other alcoholic drinks. He will be filled with the Holy Spirit, even before his birth. ¹⁶ And he will turn many Israelites to the Lord their God. ¹⁷ He will be a man with the spirit and power of Elijah. He will prepare the people for the coming of the Lord. He will turn the hearts of the fathers to their children, and he will cause those who are rebellious to accept the wisdom of the godly." ¹⁸ Zechariah said to the angel, "How can I be sure this will happen? I'm an old man now, and my wife is also well along in years." ¹⁹ Then the angel said, "I am Gabriel! I stand in the very presence of God. It was he who sent me to bring you this good news! ²⁰ But now, since you didn't believe what I said, you will be silent and unable to speak until the child is born. For my words will certainly be fulfilled at the proper time." ²¹ Meanwhile, the people were waiting for Zechariah to come out of the sanctuary, wondering why he was taking so long. ²² When he finally did come out, he couldn't speak to them. Then they realized from his gestures and his silence that he must have seen a vision in the sanctuary. ²³ When Zechariah's week of service in the Temple was over, he returned home. ²⁴ Soon afterward his wife, Elizabeth, became pregnant and went into seclusion for five months. ²⁵ "How kind the Lord is!" she exclaimed. "He has taken away my disgrace of having no children."

THE BIRTH OF JESUS FORETOLD

²⁶ In the sixth month of Elizabeth's pregnancy, God sent the angel Gabriel to Nazareth, a village in Galilee, ²⁷ to a virgin named Mary. She was engaged to be married to a man named Joseph, a descendant of King David. ²⁸ Gabriel appeared to her and said, "Greetings, favored woman! The Lord is with you!" ²⁹ Confused and disturbed, Mary tried to think what the angel could mean. ³⁰ "Don't be afraid, Mary," the angel told her, "for you have found favor with God! ³¹ You will conceive and give birth to a son, and you will name him Jesus. ³² He will be very great and will be called the Son of the Most High. The Lord God will give him the throne of his ancestor David. ³³ And he will reign over Israel forever; his Kingdom will never end!" ³⁴ Mary asked the angel, "But how can this happen? I am a virgin." ³⁵ The angel replied, "The

Holy Spirit will come upon you, and the power of the Most High will overshadow you. So the baby to be born will be holy, and he will be called the Son of God. [36] What's more, your relative Elizabeth has become pregnant in her old age! People used to say she was barren, but she has conceived a son and is now in her sixth month. [37] For the word of God will never fail." [38] Mary responded, "I am the Lord's servant. May everything you have said about me come true." And then the angel left her.

MARY VISITS ELIZABETH

[39] A few days later Mary hurried to the hill country of Judea, to the town [40] where Zechariah lived. She entered the house and greeted Elizabeth. [41] At the sound of Mary's greeting, Elizabeth's child leaped within her, and Elizabeth was filled with the Holy Spirit. [42] Elizabeth gave a glad cry and exclaimed to Mary, "God has blessed you above all women, and your child is blessed. [43] Why am I so honored, that the mother of my Lord should visit me? [44] When I heard your greeting, the baby in my womb jumped for joy. [45] You are blessed because you believed that the Lord would do what he said."

THE MAGNIFICAT: MARY'S SONG OF PRAISE

[46] Mary responded, "Oh, how my soul praises the Lord. [47] How my spirit rejoices in God my Savior! [48] For he took notice of his lowly servant girl, and from now on all generations will call me blessed. [49] For the Mighty One is holy, and he has done great things for me. [50] He shows mercy from generation to generation to all who fear him. [51] His mighty arm has done tremendous things! He has scattered the proud and haughty ones. [52] He has brought down princes from their thrones and exalted the humble. [53] He has filled the hungry with good things and sent the rich away with empty hands.

[54] He has helped his servant Israel and remembered to be merciful. [55] For he made this promise to our ancestors, to Abraham and his children forever." [56] Mary stayed with Elizabeth about three months and then went back to her own home.

THE BIRTH OF JOHN THE BAPTIST

[57] When it was time for Elizabeth's baby to be born, she gave birth to a son. [58] And when her neighbors and relatives heard that the Lord had been very merciful to her, everyone rejoiced with her. [59] When the baby was eight days old, they all came for the circumcision ceremony. They wanted to name him Zechariah, after his father. [60] But Elizabeth said, "No! His name is John!" [61] "What?" they exclaimed. "There is no one in all your family by that name." [62] So they used gestures to ask the baby's father what he wanted to name him. [63] He motioned for a writing tablet, and to everyone's surprise he wrote, "His name is John." [64] Instantly Zechariah could speak again, and he began praising God. [65] Awe fell upon the whole neighborhood, and the news of what had happened spread throughout the Judean hills. [66] Everyone who heard about it reflected on these events and asked, "What will this child turn out to be?" For the hand of the Lord was surely upon him in a special way.

ZECHARIAH'S PROPHECY

[67] Then his father, Zechariah, was filled with the Holy Spirit and gave this prophecy: [68] "Praise the Lord, the God of Israel, because he has visited and redeemed his people. [69] He has sent us a mighty Savior from the royal line of his servant David, [70] just as he promised through his holy prophets long ago. [71] Now we will be saved from our enemies and from all who hate us. [72] He has been merciful to our ancestors by remembering

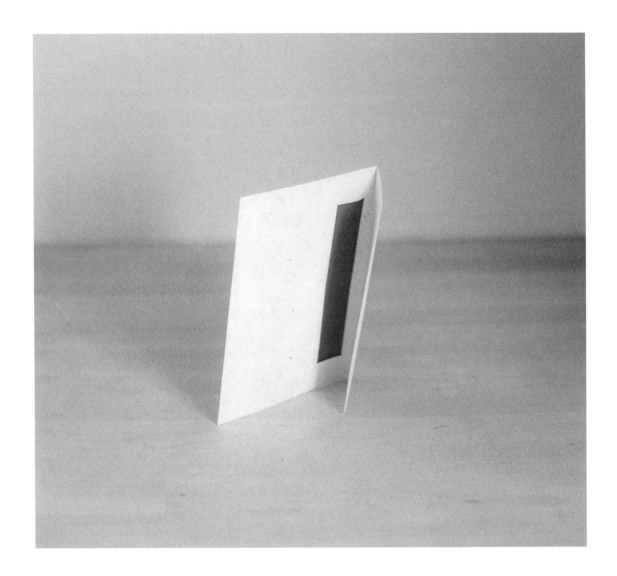

his sacred covenant—[73] the covenant he swore with an oath to our ancestor Abraham. [74] We have been rescued from our enemies so we can serve God without fear, [75] in holiness and righteousness for as long as we live. [76] And you, my little son, will be called the prophet of the Most High, because you will prepare the way for the Lord. [77] You will tell his people how to find salvation through forgiveness of their sins. [78] Because of God's tender mercy, the morning light from heaven is about to break upon us, [79] to give light to those who sit in darkness and in the shadow of death, and to guide us to the path of peace." [80] John grew up and became strong in spirit. And he lived in the wilderness until he began his public ministry to Israel.

2

THE BIRTH OF JESUS

[1] At that time the Roman emperor, Augustus, decreed that a census should be taken throughout the Roman Empire. [2] (This was the first census taken when Quirinius was governor of Syria.) [3] All returned to their own ancestral towns to register for this census. [4] And because Joseph was a descendant of King David, he had to go to Bethlehem in Judea, David's ancient home. He traveled there from the village of Nazareth in Galilee. [5] He took with him Mary, to whom he was engaged, who was now expecting a child. [6] And while they were there, the time came for her baby to be born. [7] She gave birth to her firstborn son. She wrapped him snugly in strips of cloth and laid him in a manger, because there was no lodging available for them.

THE SHEPHERDS AND ANGELS

[8] That night there were shepherds staying in the fields nearby, guarding their flocks of sheep. [9] Suddenly, an angel of the Lord appeared among them, and the radiance of the Lord's glory surrounded them. They were terrified, [10] but the angel reassured them. "Don't be afraid!" he said. "I bring you good news that will bring great joy to all people. [11] The Savior—yes, the Messiah, the Lord—has been born today in Bethlehem, the city of David! [12] And you will recognize him by this sign: You will find a baby wrapped snugly in strips of cloth, lying in a manger."

[13] Suddenly, the angel was joined by a vast host of others— the armies of heaven—praising God and saying, [14] "Glory to God in highest heaven, and peace on earth to those with whom God is pleased." [15] When the angels had re-turned to heaven, the shepherds said to each other, "Let's go to Bethlehem! Let's see this thing that has happened, which the Lord has told us about." [16] They hurried to the village and found Mary and Joseph. And there was the baby, lying in the manger. [17] After seeing him, the shepherds told everyone what had happened and what the angel had said to them about this child. [18] All who heard the shepherds' story were astonished, [19] but Mary kept all these things in her heart and thought about them often. [20] The shepherds went back to their flocks, glori-fying and praising God for all they had heard and seen. It was just as the angel had told them.

JESUS IS PRESENTED IN THE TEMPLE

[21] Eight days later, when the baby was circumcised, he was named Jesus, the name given him by the angel even before he was conceived. [22] Then it was time for their purification offering, as required by the law of Moses after the birth of a child; so his parents took him to Jerusalem to present him to the Lord. [23] The law of the Lord says, "If a woman's first child is a boy, he must be dedicated to the Lord." [24] So they offered the sacrifice required in the law of the Lord—"either a pair of turtledoves or two young pigeons."

THE PROPHECY OF SIMEON

[25] At that time there was a man in Jerusalem named Simeon. He was righteous and devout and was eagerly waiting for the Messiah to come and rescue Israel. The Holy Spirit was upon him [26] and had revealed to him that he would not die until he had seen the Lord's Messiah. [27] That day the Spirit led him to the Temple. So when Mary and Joseph came to present the baby Jesus to the Lord as the law required, [28] Simeon was there. He took the child in his arms and praised God, saying, [29] "Sovereign Lord, now let your servant die in peace, as you have promised. [30] I have seen your salvation, [31] which you have prepared for all people. [32] He is a light to reveal God to the nations, and he is the glory of your people Israel!"

[33] Jesus' parents were amazed at what was being said

about him. [34] Then Simeon blessed them, and he said to Mary, the baby's mother, "This child is destined to cause many in Israel to fall, and many others to rise. He has been sent as a sign from God, but many will oppose him. [35] As a result, the deepest thoughts of many hearts will be revealed. And a sword will pierce your very soul."

THE PROPHECY OF ANNA

[36] Anna, a prophet, was also there in the Temple. She was the daughter of Phanuel from the tribe of Asher, and she was very old. Her husband died when they had been married only seven years. [37] Then she lived as a widow to the age of eighty-four. She never left the Temple but stayed there day and night, worshiping God with fasting and prayer. [38] She came along just as Simeon was talking with Mary and Joseph, and she began praising God. She talked about the child to everyone who had been waiting expectantly for God to rescue Jerusalem. [39] When Jesus' parents had fulfilled all the requirements of the law of the Lord, they returned home to Nazareth in Galilee. [40] There the child grew up healthy and strong. He was filled with wisdom, and God's favor was on him.

JESUS SPEAKS WITH THE TEACHERS

[41] Every year Jesus' parents went to Jerusalem for the Passover festival. [42] When Jesus was twelve years old, they attended the festival as usual. [43] After the celebration was over, they started home to Nazareth, but Jesus stayed behind in Jerusalem. His parents didn't miss him at first, [44] because they assumed he was among the other travelers. But when he didn't show up that evening, they started looking for him among their relatives and friends. [45] When they couldn't find him, they went back to Jerusalem to search for him there. [46] Three days later they finally discovered him in the Temple, sitting among the religious teachers, listening to them and asking questions. [47] All who heard him were amazed at his understanding and his answers. [48] His parents didn't know what to think. "Son," his mother said to him, "why have you done this to us? Your father and I have been frantic, searching for you everywhere." [49] "But why did you need to search?" he asked. "Didn't you know that I must be in my Father's house?" [50] But they didn't understand what he meant. [51] Then he returned to Nazareth with them and was obedient to them. And his mother stored all these things in her heart. [52] Jesus grew in wisdom and in stature and in favor with God and all the people.

3

JOHN THE BAPTIST PREPARES THE WAY

[1] It was now the fifteenth year of the reign of Tiberius, the Roman emperor. Pontius Pilate was governor over Judea; Herod Antipas was ruler over Galilee; his brother Philip was ruler over Iturea and Traconitis; Lysanias was ruler over Abilene. [2] Annas and Caiaphas were the high priests. At this time a message from God came to John son of Zechariah, who was living in the wilderness. [3] Then John went from place to place on both sides of the Jordan River, preaching that people should be baptized to show that they had repented of their sins and turned to God to be forgiven. [4] Isaiah had spoken of John when he said, "He is a voice shouting in the wilderness, 'Prepare the way for the LORD's coming! Clear the road for him! [5] The valleys will be filled, and the mountains and hills made level. The curves will be straightened, and the rough places made smooth. [6] And then all people will see the salvation sent from God.'" [7] When the crowds came to John for baptism, he said, "You brood of snakes! Who warned you to flee the coming wrath? [8] Prove by the way you live that you have repented of your sins and turned to God. Don't just say to each other, 'We're safe, for we are descendants of Abraham.' That means nothing, for I tell you, God can create children of Abraham from these very stones. [9] Even now the ax of God's judgment is poised, ready to sever the roots of the trees. Yes, every tree that does not produce good fruit will be chopped down and thrown into the fire." [10] The crowds asked, "What should we do?" [11] John replied, "If you have two shirts, give one to the poor. If you have food, share it with those who are hungry." [12] Even corrupt tax collectors came to be baptized and asked, "Teacher, what should we do?" [13] He replied, "Collect no more taxes than the government requires." [14] "What should we do?" asked some soldiers. John replied, "Don't extort money or make false accusations. And be content with your pay." [15] Everyone was expecting the Messiah to come soon, and they were eager to know whether John might be the Messiah. [16] John answered their questions by saying, "I baptize you with water; but someone is coming soon who is greater than I am—so much greater that I'm not even worthy to be his slave and untie the straps of his sandals. He will baptize you with the Holy Spirit and with fire. [17] He is ready to separate the chaff from the wheat with his winnowing fork. Then he will clean up the threshing area, gathering the wheat into his barn but burning the chaff with never-ending fire." [18] John used many such warnings as he announced the Good News to the people. [19] John also publicly criticized Herod Antipas, the ruler of Galilee, for marrying Herodias, his brother's wife, and for many other wrongs he had done. [20] So Herod put John in prison, adding this sin to his many others.

THE BAPTISM OF JESUS

21 One day when the crowds were being baptized, Jesus himself was baptized. As he was praying, the heavens opened, 22 and the Holy Spirit, in bodily form, descended on him like a dove. And a voice from heaven said, "You are my dearly loved Son, and you bring me great joy."

THE ANCESTORS OF JESUS

23 Jesus was about thirty years old when he began his public ministry. Jesus was known as the son of Joseph. Joseph was the son of Heli. 24 Heli was the son of Matthat. Matthat was the son of Levi. Levi was the son of Melki. Melki was the son of Jannai. Jannai was the son of Joseph. 25 Joseph was the son of Mattathias. Mattathias was the son of Amos. Amos was the son of Nahum. Nahum was the son of Esli. Esli was the son of Naggai. 26 Naggai was the son of Maath. Maath was the son of Mattathias. Mattathias was the son of Semein. Semein was the son of Josech. Josech was the son of Joda. 27 Joda was the son of Joanan. Joanan was the son of Rhesa. Rhesa was the son of Zerubbabel. Zerubbabel was the son of Shealtiel. Shealtiel was the son of Neri. 28 Neri was the son of Melki. Melki was the son of Addi. Addi was the son of Cosam. Cosam was the son of Elmadam. Elmadam was the son of Er. 29 Er was the son of Joshua. Joshua was the son of Eliezer. Eliezer was the son of Jorim. Jorim was the son of Matthat.

Matthat was the son of Levi. 30 Levi was the son of Simeon. Simeon was the son of Judah. Judah was the son of Joseph. Joseph was the son of Jonam. Jonam was the son of Eliakim. 31 Eliakim was the son of Melea. Melea was the son of Menna. Menna was the son of Mattatha. Mattatha was the son of Nathan. Nathan was the son of David. 32 David was the son of Jesse. Jesse was the son of Obed. Obed was the son of Boaz. Boaz was the son of Salmon. Salmon was the son of Nahshon. 33 Nahshon was the son of Amminadab. Amminadab was the son of Admin. Admin was the son of Arni. Arni was the son of Hezron. Hezron was the son of Perez. Perez was the son of Judah. 34 Judah was the son of Jacob. Jacob was the son of Isaac. Isaac was the son of Abraham. Abraham was the son of Terah. Terah was the son of Nahor. 35 Nahor was the son of Serug. Serug was the son of Reu. Reu was the son of Peleg. Peleg was the son of Eber. Eber was the son of Shelah. 36 Shelah was the son of Cainan. Cainan was the son of Arphaxad. Arphaxad was the son of Shem. Shem was the son of Noah. Noah was the son of Lamech. 37 Lamech was the son of Methuselah. Methuselah was the son of Enoch. Enoch was the son of Jared. Jared was the son of Mahalalel. Mahalalel was the son of Kenan. 38 Kenan was the son of Enosh. Enosh was the son of Seth. Seth was the son of Adam. Adam was the son of God.

4

THE TEMPTATION OF JESUS

¹ Then Jesus, full of the Holy Spirit, returned from the Jordan River. He was led by the Spirit in the wilderness, ² where he was tempted by the devil for forty days. Jesus ate nothing all that time and became very hungry. ³ Then the devil said to him, "If you are the Son of God, tell this stone to become a loaf of bread." ⁴ But Jesus told him, "No! The Scriptures say, 'People do not live by bread alone.'" ⁵ Then the devil took him up and revealed to him all the kingdoms of the world in a moment of time. ⁶ "I will give you the glory of these kingdoms and authority over them," the devil said, "because they are mine to give to anyone I please. ⁷ I will give it all to you if you will worship me." ⁸ Jesus replied, "The Scriptures say, 'You must worship the Lᴏʀᴅ your God and serve only him.'" ⁹ Then the devil took him to Jerusalem, to the highest point of the Temple, and said, "If you are the Son of God, jump off! ¹⁰ For the Scriptures say, 'He will order his angels to protect and guard you. ¹¹ And they will hold you up with their hands so you won't even hurt your foot on a stone.'" ¹² Jesus responded, "The Scriptures also say, 'You must not test the Lᴏʀᴅ your God.'" ¹³ When the devil had finished tempting Jesus, he left him until the next opportunity came.

THE TEMPTATION OF JESUS

LUKE 4:1-13

READ

1. Read Luke 4:1-13 slowly (aloud, if it's not intrusive to others).
2. Look at the photo on page 18.
3. Pause.

REFLECT

1. Read the passage again, slowly.
2. Notice the details of the photo:
   - how the hands are reaching and grasping
   - what each hand is holding or doing and what those objects and actions represent
   - the darkness behind it all
3. If the photo included a hand grasping something that tempts you, what might that be?
4. Even if wealth, admiration, and having a voice tempted Jesus, his response was in essence, "This is not who I am. I don't really want those things."
5. What, if anything, do you sense God inviting you to consider?

RESPOND

1. Position your hand as in the photo as if holding something that tempts you.
2. Ask God to show you who you are and what you really want.
3. Say (aloud, if possible) what you sense coming to you. What might God want you to know?
4. Open your hand to let go of the object, even if at this moment you'd like to hold on to it.

REST

1. Exhale.
2. Drop your hands to your side or your lap to indicate that you are at peace, that you are fully satisfied and don't need anything else besides what you have.

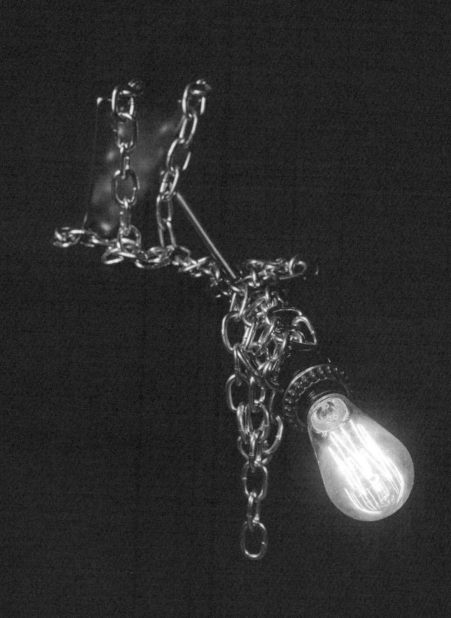

JESUS REJECTED AT NAZARETH

[14] Then Jesus returned to Galilee, filled with the Holy Spirit's power. Reports about him spread quickly through the whole region. [15] He taught regularly in their synagogues and was praised by everyone. [16] When he came to the village of Nazareth, his boyhood home, he went as usual to the synagogue on the Sabbath and stood up to read the Scriptures. [17] The scroll of Isaiah the prophet was handed to him. He unrolled the scroll and found the place where this was written: [18] "The Spirit of the LORD is upon me, for he has anointed me to bring Good News to the poor. He has sent me to proclaim that captives will be released, that the blind will see, that the oppressed will be set free, [19] and that the time of the LORD's favor has come." [20] He rolled up the scroll, handed it back to the attendant, and sat down. All eyes in the synagogue looked at him intently. [21] Then he began to speak to them. "The Scripture you've just heard has been fulfilled this very day!" [22] Everyone spoke well of him and was amazed by the gracious words that came from his lips. "How can this be?" they asked. "Isn't this Joseph's son?" [23] Then he said, "You will undoubtedly quote me this proverb: 'Physician, heal yourself'—meaning, 'Do miracles here in your hometown like those you did in Capernaum.' [24] But I tell you the truth, no prophet is accepted in his own hometown. [25] Certainly there were many needy widows in Israel in Elijah's time, when the heavens were closed for three and a half years, and a severe famine devastated the land. [26] Yet Elijah was not sent to any of them. He was sent instead to a foreigner—a widow of Zarephath in the land of Sidon. [27] And many in Israel had leprosy in the time of the prophet Elisha, but the only one healed was Naaman, a Syrian." [28] When they heard this, the people in the synagogue were furious. [29] Jumping up, they mobbed him and forced him to the edge of the hill on which the town was built. They intended to push him over the cliff, [30] but he passed right through the crowd and went on his way.

JESUS CASTS OUT A DEMON

[31] Then Jesus went to Capernaum, a town in Galilee, and taught there in the synagogue every Sabbath day. [32] There, too, the people were amazed at his teaching, for he spoke with authority. [33] Once when he was in the synagogue, a man possessed by a demon—an evil spirit—cried out, shouting, [34] "Go away! Why are you interfering with us, Jesus of Nazareth? Have you come to destroy us? I know who you are—the Holy One of God!" [35] But Jesus reprimanded him. "Be quiet! Come out of the man," he ordered. At that, the demon threw the man to the floor as the crowd watched; then it came out of him without hurting him further. [36] Amazed, the people exclaimed, "What authority and power this man's words possess! Even evil spirits obey him, and they flee at his command!" [37] The news about Jesus spread through every village in the entire region.

JESUS HEALS MANY PEOPLE

[38] After leaving the synagogue that day, Jesus went to Simon's home, where he found Simon's mother-in-law very sick with a high fever. "Please heal her," everyone begged. [39] Standing at her bedside, he rebuked the fever, and it left her. And she got up at once and prepared a meal for them. [40] As the sun went down that evening, people throughout the village brought sick family members to Jesus. No matter what their diseases were, the touch of his hand healed every one. [41] Many were possessed by demons; and the demons came out at his command, shouting, "You are the Son of God!" But because they knew he was the Messiah, he rebuked them and refused to let them speak.

JESUS CONTINUES TO PREACH

[42] Early the next morning Jesus went out to an isolated place. The crowds searched everywhere for him, and when they finally found him, they begged him not to leave them. [43] But he replied, "I must preach the Good News of the Kingdom of God in other towns, too, because that is why I was sent." [44] So he continued to travel around, preaching in synagogues throughout Judea.

5

THE FIRST DISCIPLES

[1] One day as Jesus was preaching on the shore of the Sea of Galilee, great crowds pressed in on him to listen to the word of God. [2] He noticed two empty boats at the water's edge, for the fishermen had left them and were washing their nets. [3] Stepping into one of the boats, Jesus asked Simon, its owner, to push it out into the water. So he sat in the boat and taught the crowds from there. [4] When he had finished speaking, he said to Simon, "Now go out where it is deeper, and let down your nets to catch some fish." [5] "Master," Simon replied, "we worked hard all last night and didn't catch a thing. But if you say so, I'll let the nets down again." [6] And this time their nets were so full of fish they began to tear! [7] A shout for help brought their partners in the other boat, and soon both boats were filled with fish and on the verge of sinking. [8] When Simon Peter realized what had happened, he fell to his knees before Jesus and said, "Oh, Lord, please leave me—I'm such a sinful man." [9] For he was awestruck by the number of fish they had caught, as were the others with him. [10] His partners, James and John, the sons of Zebedee, were also amazed. Jesus replied to Simon, "Don't be afraid! From now on you'll be fishing for people!" [11] And as soon as they landed, they left everything and followed Jesus.

THE FIRST DISCIPLES

LUKE 5:1-11

READ

1. Read Luke 5:1-11 slowly (aloud, if it's not intrusive to others).
2. Look at the photo on page 22.
3. Pause.

REFLECT

1. Read the passage again, slowly. Notice the arc of Peter's feelings: from hesitant to "go out where it is deeper" to falling on his knees in the boat, and once ashore leaving everything to follow Jesus.
2. Notice the details of the photo. Which stands out to you?
   - the shadowed figure letting go of the fishing nets (the tools of the trade, the means of making a living)
   - the bowed head of each figure
   - the open arms and hands of the figure in the foreground
3. Read the passage again. What word or phrase stands out to you?

4. What, if anything, in this passage do you find that you want for yourself?

RESPOND

1. Say aloud to God what you most need to say at this point—to ask for, to protest, to be open to, to relax in.
2. As you pray, you may wish to take on the posture of one of the figures in the photo.
3. If you're willing, ask God for what you would most like to open yourself up to.
4. Open your hands to embrace that.

REST

1. Exhale.
2. Soak in the idea that you can be a simple disciple—one who is progressively becoming more like your Teacher—and do the things your Master invites you into.

JESUS HEALS A MAN WITH LEPROSY

12 In one of the villages, Jesus met a man with an advanced case of leprosy. When the man saw Jesus, he bowed with his face to the ground, begging to be healed. "Lord," he said, "if you are willing, you can heal me and make me clean." 13 Jesus reached out and touched him. "I am willing," he said. "Be healed!" And instantly the leprosy disappeared. 14 Then Jesus instructed him not to tell anyone what had happened. He said, "Go to the priest and let him examine you. Take along the offering required in the law of Moses for those who have been healed of leprosy. This will be a public testimony that you have been cleansed." 15 But despite Jesus' instructions, the report of his power spread even faster, and vast crowds came to hear him preach and to be healed of their diseases. 16 But Jesus often withdrew to the wilderness for prayer.

JESUS HEALS A PARALYZED MAN

[17] One day while Jesus was teaching, some Pharisees and teachers of religious law were sitting nearby. (It seemed that these men showed up from every village in all Galilee and Judea, as well as from Jerusalem.) And the Lord's healing power was strongly with Jesus. [18] Some men came carrying a paralyzed man on a sleeping mat. They tried to take him inside to Jesus, [19] but they couldn't reach him because of the crowd. So they went up to the roof and took off some tiles. Then they lowered the sick man on his mat down into the crowd, right in front of Jesus. [20] Seeing their faith, Jesus said to the man, "Young man, your sins are forgiven." [21] But the Pharisees and teachers of religious law said to themselves, "Who does he think he is? That's blasphemy! Only God can forgive sins!" [22] Jesus knew what they were thinking, so he asked them, "Why do you question this in your hearts? [23] Is it easier to say 'Your sins are forgiven,' or 'Stand up and walk'? [24] So I will prove to you that the Son of Man has the authority on earth to forgive sins." Then Jesus turned to the paralyzed man and said, "Stand up, pick up your mat, and go home!" [25] And immediately, as everyone watched, the man jumped up, picked up his mat, and went home praising God. [26] Everyone was gripped with great wonder and awe, and they praised God, exclaiming, "We have seen amazing things today!"

JESUS CALLS LEVI (MATTHEW)

²⁷ Later, as Jesus left the town, he saw a tax collector named Levi sitting at his tax collector's booth. "Follow me and be my disciple," Jesus said to him. ²⁸ So Levi got up, left everything, and followed him. ²⁹ Later, Levi held a banquet in his home with Jesus as the guest of honor. Many of Levi's fellow tax collectors and other guests also ate with them. ³⁰ But the Pharisees and their teachers of religious law complained bitterly to Jesus' disciples, "Why do you eat and drink with such scum?" ³¹ Jesus answered them, "Healthy people don't need a doctor—sick people do. ³² I have come to call not those who think they are righteous, but those who know they are sinners and need to repent."

A DISCUSSION ABOUT FASTING

³³ One day some people said to Jesus, "John the Baptist's disciples fast and pray regularly, and so do the disciples of the Pharisees. Why are your disciples always eating and drinking?" ³⁴ Jesus responded, "Do wedding guests fast while celebrating with the groom? Of course not. ³⁵ But someday the groom will be taken away from them, and then they will fast." ³⁶ Then Jesus gave them this illustration: "No one tears a piece of cloth from a new garment and uses it to patch an old garment. For then the new garment would be ruined, and the new patch wouldn't even match the old garment. ³⁷ And no one puts new wine into old wineskins. For the new wine would burst the wineskins, spilling the wine and ruining the skins. ³⁸ New wine must be stored in new wineskins. ³⁹ But no one who drinks the old wine seems to want the new wine. 'The old is just fine,' they say."

6

A DISCUSSION ABOUT THE SABBATH

[1] One Sabbath day as Jesus was walking through some grainfields, his disciples broke off heads of grain, rubbed off the husks in their hands, and ate the grain. [2] But some Pharisees said, "Why are you breaking the law by harvesting grain on the Sabbath?" [3] Jesus replied, "Haven't you read in the Scriptures what David did when he and his companions were hungry? [4] He went into the house of God and broke the law by eating the sacred loaves of bread that only the priests can eat. He also gave some to his companions." [5] And Jesus added, "The Son of Man is Lord, even over the Sabbath."

JESUS HEALS ON THE SABBATH

[6] On another Sabbath day, a man with a deformed right hand was in the synagogue while Jesus was teaching. [7] The teachers of religious law and the Pharisees watched Jesus closely. If he healed the man's hand, they planned to accuse him of working on the Sabbath. [8] But Jesus knew their thoughts. He said to the man with the deformed hand, "Come and stand in front of everyone." So the man came forward. [9] Then Jesus said to his critics, "I have a question for you. Does the law permit good deeds on the Sabbath, or is it a day for doing evil? Is this a day to save life or to destroy it?" [10] He looked around at them one by one and then said to the man, "Hold out your hand." So the man held out his hand, and it was restored! [11] At this, the enemies of Jesus were wild with rage and began to discuss what to do with him.

JESUS CHOOSES THE TWELVE APOSTLES

[12] One day soon afterward Jesus went up on a mountain to pray, and he prayed to God all night. [13] At daybreak he called together all of his disciples and chose twelve of them to be apostles. Here are their names: [14] Simon (whom he named Peter), Andrew (Peter's brother), James, John, Philip, Bartholomew, [15] Matthew, Thomas, James (son of Alphaeus), Simon (who was called the zealot), [16] Judas (son of James), Judas Iscariot (who later betrayed him).

CROWDS FOLLOW JESUS

[17] When they came down from the mountain, the disciples stood with Jesus on a large, level area, surrounded by many of his followers and by the crowds. There were people from all over Judea and from Jerusalem and from as far north as the seacoasts of Tyre and Sidon. [18] They had come to hear him and to be healed of their diseases; and those troubled by evil spirits were healed. [19] Everyone tried to touch him, because healing power went out from him, and he healed everyone.

THE BEATITUDES

[20] Then Jesus turned to his disciples and said, "God blesses you who are poor, for the Kingdom of God is yours. [21] God blesses you who are hungry now, for you will be satisfied. God blesses you who weep now, for in due time you will laugh. [22] What blessings await you when people hate you and exclude you and mock you and curse you as evil because you follow the Son of Man. [23] When that happens, be happy! Yes, leap for joy! For a great reward awaits you in heaven. And remember, their ancestors treated the ancient prophets that same way.

SORROWS FORETOLD

[24] "What sorrow awaits you who are rich, for you have your only happiness now. [25] What sorrow awaits you who are fat and prosperous now, for a time of awful hunger awaits you. What sorrow awaits you who laugh now, for your laughing will turn to mourning and sorrow. [26] What sorrow awaits you who are praised by the crowds, for their ancestors also praised false prophets.

LOVE FOR ENEMIES

[27] "But to you who are willing to listen, I say, love your enemies! Do good to those who hate you. [28] Bless those who curse you. Pray for those who hurt you. [29] If someone slaps you on one cheek, offer the other cheek also. If someone demands your coat, offer your shirt also. [30] Give to anyone who asks; and when things are taken away from you, don't try to get them back. [31] Do to others as you would like them to do to you. [32] If you love only those who love you, why should you get credit for that? Even sinners love those who love them! [33] And if you do good only to those who do good to you, why should you get credit? Even sinners do that much! [34] And if you lend money only to those who can repay you, why should you get credit? Even sinners will lend to other sinners for a full return. [35] Love your enemies! Do good to them. Lend to them without expecting to be repaid. Then your reward from heaven will be very great, and you will truly be acting as children of the Most High, for he is kind to those who are unthankful and wicked. [36] You must be compassionate, just as your Father is compassionate.

DO NOT JUDGE OTHERS

[37] "Do not judge others, and you will not be judged. Do not condemn others, or it will all come back against you. Forgive others, and you will be forgiven. [38] Give, and you will receive. Your gift will return to you in full—pressed down, shaken together to make room for more, running over, and poured into your lap. The amount you give will determine the amount you get back." [39] Then Jesus gave the following illustration: "Can one blind person lead another? Won't they both fall into a ditch? [40] Students are not greater than their teacher. But the student who is fully trained will become like the teacher. [41] And why worry about a speck in your friend's eye when you have a log in your own? [42] How can you think of saying, 'Friend, let me help you get rid of that speck in your eye,' when you can't see past the log in your own eye? Hypocrite! First get rid of the log in your own eye; then you will see well enough to deal with the speck in your friend's eye.

THE TREE AND ITS FRUIT

[43] "A good tree can't produce bad fruit, and a bad tree can't produce good fruit. [44] A tree is identified by its fruit. Figs are never gathered from thornbushes, and grapes are not picked from bramble bushes. [45] A good person produces good things from the treasury of a good heart, and an evil person produces evil things from the treasury of an evil heart. What you say flows from what is in your heart.

BUILDING ON A SOLID FOUNDATION

46 "So why do you keep calling me 'Lord, Lord!' when you don't do what I say? 47 I will show you what it's like when someone comes to me, listens to my teaching, and then follows it. 48 It is like a person building a house who digs deep and lays the foundation on solid rock. When the floodwaters rise and break against that house, it stands firm because it is well built. 49 But anyone who hears and doesn't obey is like a person who builds a house right on the ground, without a foundation. When the floods sweep down against that house, it will collapse into a heap of ruins."

7

THE FAITH OF A ROMAN OFFICER

[1] When Jesus had finished saying all this to the people, he returned to Capernaum. [2] At that time the highly valued slave of a Roman officer was sick and near death. [3] When the officer heard about Jesus, he sent some respected Jewish elders to ask him to come and heal his slave. [4] So they earnestly begged Jesus to help the man. "If anyone deserves your help, he does," they said, [5] "for he loves the Jewish people and even built a synagogue for us." [6] So Jesus went with them. But just before they arrived at the house, the officer sent some friends to say, "Lord, don't trouble yourself by coming to my home, for I am not worthy of such an honor. [7] I am not even worthy to come and meet you. Just say the word from where you are, and my servant will be healed. [8] I know this because I am under the authority of my superior officers, and I have authority over my soldiers. I only need to say, 'Go,' and they go, or 'Come,' and they come. And if I say to my slaves, 'Do this,' they do it." [9] When Jesus heard this, he was amazed. Turning to the crowd that was following him, he said, "I tell you, I haven't seen faith like this in all Israel!" [10] And when the officer's friends returned to his house, they found the slave completely healed.

JESUS RAISES A WIDOW'S SON

[11] Soon afterward Jesus went with his disciples to the village of Nain, and a large crowd followed him. [12] A funeral procession was coming out as he approached the village gate. The young man who had died was a widow's only son, and a large crowd from the village was with her. [13] When the Lord saw her, his heart overflowed with compassion. "Don't cry!" he said. [14] Then he walked over to the coffin and touched it, and the bearers stopped. "Young man," he said, "I tell you, get up." [15] Then the dead boy sat up and began to talk! And Jesus gave him back to his mother. [16] Great fear swept the crowd, and they praised God, saying, "A mighty prophet has risen among us," and "God has visited his people today." [17] And the news about Jesus spread throughout Judea and the surrounding countryside.

JESUS AND JOHN THE BAPTIST

[18] The disciples of John the Baptist told John about everything Jesus was doing. So John called for two of his disciples, [19] and he sent them to the Lord to ask him, "Are you the Messiah we've been expecting, or should we keep looking for someone else?" [20] John's two disciples found Jesus and said to him, "John the Baptist sent us to ask, 'Are you the Messiah we've been expecting, or should we keep looking for someone else?'" [21] At that very time, Jesus cured many people of their diseases, illnesses, and evil spirits, and he restored sight to many who were blind. [22] Then he told John's disciples, "Go back to John and tell him what you have seen and heard—the blind see, the lame walk, those with leprosy are cured, the deaf hear, the dead are raised to life, and the Good News is being preached to the poor." [23] And he added, "God blesses those who do not fall away because of me." [24] After John's disciples left, Jesus began talking about him to the crowds. "What kind of man did you go into the wilderness to see? Was he a weak reed, swayed by every breath of wind? [25] Or were you expecting to see a man dressed in expensive clothes? No, people who wear beautiful clothes and live in luxury are found in palaces. [26] Were you looking for a prophet? Yes, and he is more than a prophet. [27] John is the man to whom the Scriptures refer when they say, 'Look, I am sending my messenger ahead of you, and he will prepare your way before you.' [28] I tell you, of all who have ever lived, none is greater than John. Yet even the least person in the Kingdom of God is greater than he is!" [29] When they heard this, all the people—even the tax collectors—agreed that God's way was right, for they had been baptized by John. [30] But the Pharisees and experts in religious law rejected God's plan for them, for they had refused John's baptism. [31] "To what can I compare the people of this generation?" Jesus asked. "How can I describe them? [32] They are like children playing a game in the public square. They complain to their friends, 'We played wedding songs, and you didn't dance, so we played funeral songs, and you didn't weep.' [33] For John the Baptist didn't spend his time eating bread or drinking wine, and you say, 'He's possessed by a demon.' [34] The Son of Man, on the other hand, feasts and drinks, and you say, 'He's a glutton and a drunkard, and a friend of tax collectors and other sinners!' [35] But wisdom is shown to be right by the lives of those who follow it."

JESUS ANOINTED BY A SINFUL WOMAN

LUKE 7:36-50

READ

1. Read Luke 7:36-50 slowly (aloud, if it's not intrusive to others).
2. Look at the photo on page 39.
3. Pause.

REFLECT

1. In the passage, the immoral woman generously blesses Jesus by washing his feet with expensive perfume. But in the photo, the woman is the one being generously blessed.
2. Read verses 44-47 aloud slowly as if Jesus was saying them to an esteemed, important leader today. Continue by reading verses 48-50 aloud as if Jesus was saying them to a notorious woman today.
3. How do you think Jesus felt saying those things?
4. How do you think the woman felt when he publicly described how she had blessed him, formally forgave her sins, and said that it was her own faith that saved her?

5. Ask God where you are situated today: as the blesser or the one being blessed.
6. What, if anything, do you sense God inviting you to consider?

RESPOND

1. Position your hands as in the photo as if receiving a blessing from God.
2. Allow a few minutes to gain a sense of blessing from head to toe.
3. You may wish to respond aloud or simply continue holding out your hands as a prayer of thanks.

REST

1. Soak in the thought that we bless God (by offering affectionate and grateful praise), as in the line "Bless the LORD, O my soul" (Psalm 103:1 NRSV).
2. Rest in the thought that we receive generous blessings from God.

JESUS ANOINTED BY A SINFUL WOMAN

[36] One of the Pharisees asked Jesus to have dinner with him, so Jesus went to his home and sat down to eat. [37] When a certain immoral woman from that city heard he was eating there, she brought a beautiful alabaster jar filled with expensive perfume. [38] Then she knelt behind him at his feet, weeping. Her tears fell on his feet, and she wiped them off with her hair. Then she kept kissing his feet and putting perfume on them. [39] When the Pharisee who had invited him saw this, he said to himself, "If this man were a prophet, he would know what kind of woman is touching him. She's a sinner!" [40] Then Jesus answered his thoughts. "Simon," he said to the Pharisee, "I have something to say to you." "Go ahead, Teacher," Simon replied. [41] Then Jesus told him this story: "A man loaned money to two people—500 pieces of silver to one and 50 pieces to the other. [42] But neither of them could repay him, so he kindly forgave them both, canceling their debts. Who do you suppose loved him more after that?" [43] Simon answered, "I suppose the one for whom he canceled the larger debt." "That's right," Jesus said.

[44] Then he turned to the woman and said to Simon, "Look at this woman kneeling here. When I entered your home, you didn't offer me water to wash the dust from my feet, but she has washed them with her tears and wiped them with her hair. [45] You didn't greet me with a kiss, but from the time I first came in, she has not stopped kissing my feet. [46] You neglected the courtesy of olive oil to anoint my head, but she has anointed my feet with rare perfume. [47] I tell you, her sins—and they are many—have been forgiven, so she has shown me much love. But a person who is forgiven little shows only little love." [48] Then Jesus said to the woman, "Your sins are forgiven." [49] The men at the table said among themselves, "Who is this man, that he goes around forgiving sins?" [50] And Jesus said to the woman, "Your faith has saved you; go in peace."

8

WOMEN WHO FOLLOWED JESUS

[1] Soon afterward Jesus began a tour of the nearby towns and villages, preaching and announcing the Good News about the Kingdom of God. He took his twelve disciples with him, [2] along with some women who had been cured of evil spirits and diseases. Among them were Mary Magdalene, from whom he had cast out seven demons; [3] Joanna, the wife of Chuza, Herod's business manager; Susanna; and many others who were contributing from their own resources to support Jesus and his disciples.

PARABLE OF THE FARMER SCATTERING SEED

[4] One day Jesus told a story in the form of a parable to a large crowd that had gathered from many towns to hear him: [5] "A farmer went out to plant his seed. As he scattered it across his field, some seed fell on a footpath, where it was stepped on, and the birds ate it. [6] Other seed fell among rocks. It began to grow, but the plant soon wilted and died for lack of moisture. [7] Other seed fell among thorns that grew up with it and choked out the tender plants. [8] Still other seed fell on fertile soil. This seed grew and produced a crop that was a hundred times as much as had been planted!" When he had said this, he called out, "Anyone with ears to hear should listen and understand." [9] His disciples asked him what this parable meant. [10] He replied, "You are permitted to understand the secrets of the Kingdom of God. But I use parables to teach the others so that the Scriptures might be fulfilled: 'When they look, they won't really see. When they hear, they won't understand.' [11] This is the meaning of the parable: The seed is God's word. [12] The seeds that fell on the footpath represent those who hear the message, only to have the devil come and take it away from their hearts and prevent them from believing and being saved. [13] The seeds on the rocky soil represent those who hear the message and receive it with joy. But since they don't have deep roots, they believe for a while, then they fall away when they face temptation. [14] The seeds that fell among the thorns represent those who hear the message, but all too quickly the message is crowded out by the cares and riches and pleasures of this life. And so they never grow into maturity. [15] And the seeds that fell on the good soil represent honest, good-hearted people who hear God's word, cling to it, and patiently produce a huge harvest.

PARABLE OF THE LAMP

[16] "No one lights a lamp and then covers it with a bowl or hides it under a bed. A lamp is placed on a stand, where its light can be seen by all who enter the house. [17] For all that is secret will eventually be brought into the open, and everything that is concealed will be brought to light and made known to all. [18] So pay attention to how you hear. To those who listen to my teaching, more understanding will be given. But for those who are not listening, even what they think they understand will be taken away from them."

THE TRUE FAMILY OF JESUS

[19] Then Jesus' mother and brothers came to see him, but they couldn't get to him because of the crowd. [20] Someone told Jesus, "Your mother and your brothers are standing outside, and they want to see you." [21] Jesus replied, "My mother and my brothers are all those who hear God's word and obey it."

JESUS CALMS THE STORM

[22] One day Jesus said to his disciples, "Let's cross to the other side of the lake." So they got into a boat and started out. [23] As they sailed across, Jesus settled down for a nap. But soon a fierce storm came down on the lake. The boat was filling with water, and they were in real danger. [24] The disciples went and woke him up, shouting, "Master, Master, we're going to drown!" When Jesus woke up, he rebuked the wind and the raging waves. Suddenly the storm stopped and all was calm. [25] Then he asked them, "Where is your faith?" The disciples were terrified and amazed. "Who is this man?" they asked each other. "When he gives a command, even the wind and waves obey him!"

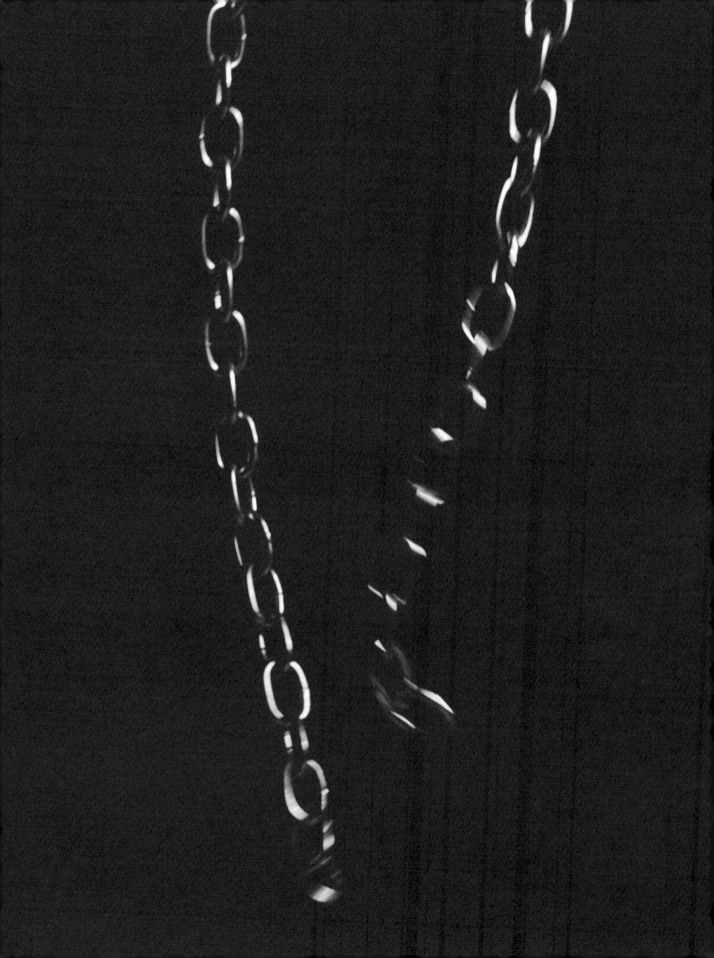

JESUS HEALS A DEMON-POSSESSED MAN

[26] So they arrived in the region of the Gerasenes, across the lake from Galilee. [27] As Jesus was climbing out of the boat, a man who was possessed by demons came out to meet him. For a long time he had been homeless and naked, living in the tombs outside the town. [28] As soon as he saw Jesus, he shrieked and fell down in front of him. Then he screamed, "Why are you interfering with me, Jesus, Son of the Most High God? Please, I beg you, don't torture me!" [29] For Jesus had already commanded the evil spirit to come out of him. This spirit had often taken control of the man. Even when he was placed under guard and put in chains and shackles, he simply broke them and rushed out into the wilderness, completely under the demon's power. [30] Jesus demanded, "What is your name?" "Legion," he replied, for he was filled with many demons. [31] The demons kept begging Jesus not to send them into the bottomless pit. [32] There happened to be a large herd of pigs feeding on the hillside nearby, and the demons begged him to let them enter into the pigs. So Jesus gave them permission. [33] Then the demons came out of the man and entered the pigs, and the entire herd plunged down the steep hillside into the lake and drowned. [34] When the herdsmen saw it, they fled to the nearby town and the surrounding countryside, spreading the news as they ran. [35] People rushed out to see what had happened. A crowd soon gathered around Jesus, and they saw the man who had been freed from the demons. He was sitting at Jesus' feet, fully clothed and perfectly sane, and they were all afraid. [36] Then those who had seen what happened told the others how the demon-possessed man had been healed. [37] And all the people in the region of the Gerasenes begged Jesus to go away and leave them alone, for a great wave of fear swept over them. So Jesus returned to the boat and left, crossing back to the other side of the lake. [38] The man who had been freed from the demons begged to go with him. But Jesus sent him home, saying, [39] "No, go back to your family, and tell them everything God has done for you." So he went all through the town proclaiming the great things Jesus had done for him.

JESUS HEALS IN RESPONSE TO FAITH

[40] On the other side of the lake the crowds welcomed Jesus, because they had been waiting for him. [41] Then a man named Jairus, a leader of the local synagogue, came and fell at Jesus' feet, pleading with him to come home with him. [42] His only daughter, who was about twelve years old, was dying. As Jesus went with him, he was surrounded by the crowds. [43] A woman in the crowd had suffered for twelve years with constant bleeding, and she could find no cure. [44] Coming up behind Jesus, she touched the fringe of his robe. Immediately, the bleeding stopped. [45] "Who touched me?" Jesus asked. Everyone denied it, and Peter said, "Master, this whole crowd is pressing up against you." [46] But Jesus said, "Someone deliberately touched me, for I felt healing power go out from me." [47] When the woman realized that she could not stay hidden, she began to tremble and fell to her knees in front of him. The whole crowd heard her explain why she had touched him and that she had been immediately healed. [48] "Daughter," he said to her, "your faith has made you well. Go in peace." [49] While he was still speaking to her, a messenger arrived from the home of Jairus, the leader of the synagogue. He told him, "Your daughter is dead. There's no use troubling the Teacher now." [50] But when Jesus heard what had happened, he said to Jairus, "Don't be afraid. Just have faith, and she will be healed." [51] When they arrived at the house, Jesus wouldn't let anyone go in with him except Peter, John, James, and the little girl's father and mother. [52] The house was filled with people weeping and wailing, but he said, "Stop the weeping! She isn't dead; she's only asleep." [53] But the crowd laughed at him because they all knew she had died. [54] Then Jesus took her by the hand and said in a loud voice, "My child, get up!" [55] And at that moment her life returned, and she immediately stood up! Then Jesus told them to give her something to eat. [56] Her parents were overwhelmed, but Jesus insisted that they not tell anyone what had happened.

9

JESUS SENDS OUT THE TWELVE DISCIPLES

[1] One day Jesus called together his twelve disciples and gave them power and authority to cast out all demons and to heal all diseases. [2] Then he sent them out to tell everyone about the Kingdom of God and to heal the sick. [3] "Take nothing for your journey," he instructed them. "Don't take a walking stick, a traveler's bag, food, money, or even a change of clothes. [4] Wherever you go, stay in the same house until you leave town. [5] And if a town refuses to welcome you, shake its dust from your feet as you leave to show that you have abandoned those people to their fate." [6] So they began their circuit of the villages, preaching the Good News and healing the sick.

HEROD'S CONFUSION

[7] When Herod Antipas, the ruler of Galilee, heard about everything Jesus was doing, he was puzzled. Some were saying that John the Baptist had been raised from the dead. [8] Others thought Jesus was Elijah or one of the other prophets risen from the dead. [9] "I beheaded John," Herod said, "so who is this man about whom I hear such stories?" And he kept trying to see him.

JESUS FEEDS FIVE THOUSAND

[10] When the apostles returned, they told Jesus everything they had done. Then he slipped quietly away with them toward the town of Bethsaida. [11] But the crowds found out where he was going, and they followed him. He welcomed them and taught them about the Kingdom of God, and he healed those who were sick. [12] Late in the afternoon the twelve disciples came to him and said, "Send the crowds away to the nearby villages and farms, so they can find food and lodging for the night. There is nothing to eat here in this remote place." [13] But Jesus said, "You feed them." "But we have only five loaves of bread and two fish," they answered. "Or are you expecting us to go and buy enough food for this whole crowd?" [14] For there were about 5,000 men there. Jesus replied, "Tell them to sit down in groups of about fifty each." [15] So the people all sat down. [16] Jesus took the five loaves and two fish, looked up toward heaven, and blessed them. Then, breaking the loaves into pieces, he kept giving the bread and fish to the disciples so they could distribute it to the people. [17] They all ate as much as they wanted, and afterward, the disciples picked up twelve baskets of leftovers!

PETER'S DECLARATION ABOUT JESUS

[18] One day Jesus left the crowds to pray alone. Only his disciples were with him, and he asked them, "Who do people say I am?" [19] "Well," they replied, "some say John the Baptist, some say Elijah, and others say you are one of the other ancient prophets risen from the dead." [20] Then he asked them, "But who do you say I am?" Peter replied, "You are the Messiah sent from God!"

JESUS PREDICTS HIS DEATH

[21] Jesus warned his disciples not to tell anyone who he was. [22] "The Son of Man must suffer many terrible things," he said. "He will be rejected by the elders, the leading priests, and the teachers of religious law. He will be killed, but on the third day he will be raised from the dead." [23] Then he said to the crowd, "If any of you wants to be my follower, you must give up your own way, take up your cross daily, and follow me. [24] If you try to hang on to your life, you will lose it. But if you give up your life for my sake, you will save it. [25] And what do you benefit if you gain the whole world but are yourself lost or destroyed? [26] If anyone is ashamed of me and my message, the Son of Man will be ashamed of that person when he returns in his glory and in the glory of the Father and the holy angels. [27] I tell you the truth, some standing here right now will not die before they see the Kingdom of God."

THE TRANSFIGURATION

[28] About eight days later Jesus took Peter, John, and James up on a mountain to pray. [29] And as he was praying, the appearance of his face was transformed, and his clothes became dazzling white. [30] Suddenly, two men, Moses and Elijah, appeared and began talking with Jesus. [31] They were glorious to see. And they were speaking about his exodus from this world, which was about to be fulfilled in Jerusalem. [32] Peter and the others had fallen asleep. When they woke up, they saw Jesus' glory and the two men standing with him. [33] As Moses and Elijah were starting to leave, Peter, not even knowing what he was saying, blurted out, "Master, it's wonderful for us to be here! Let's make three shelters as memorials —one for you, one for Moses, and one for Elijah." [34] But even as he was saying this, a cloud overshadowed them, and terror gripped them as the cloud covered them. [35] Then a voice from the cloud said, "This is my Son, my Chosen One. Listen to him." [36] When the voice finished, Jesus was there alone. They didn't tell anyone at that time what they had seen.

JESUS HEALS A DEMON-POSSESSED BOY

[37] The next day, after they had come down the mountain, a large crowd met Jesus. [38] A man in the crowd called out to him, "Teacher, I beg you to look at my son, my only child. [39] An evil spirit keeps seizing him, making him scream. It throws him into convulsions so that he foams at the mouth. It batters him and hardly ever leaves him alone. [40] I begged your disciples to cast out the spirit, but they couldn't do it." [41] Jesus said, "You faithless and corrupt people! How long must I be with you and put up with you?" Then he said to the man, "Bring your son here." [42] As the boy came forward, the demon knocked him to the ground and threw him into a violent convulsion. But Jesus rebuked the evil spirit and healed the boy. Then he gave him back to his father. [43] Awe gripped the people as they saw this majestic display of God's power.

JESUS AGAIN PREDICTS HIS DEATH

While everyone was marveling at everything he was doing, Jesus said to his disciples, [44] "Listen to me and remember what I say. The Son of Man is going to be betrayed into the hands of his enemies." [45] But they didn't know what he meant. Its significance was hidden from them, so they couldn't understand it, and they were afraid to ask him about it.

THE GREATEST IN THE KINGDOM

[46] Then his disciples began arguing about which of them was the greatest. [47] But Jesus knew their thoughts, so he brought a little child to his side. [48] Then he said to them, "Anyone who welcomes a little child like this on my behalf welcomes me, and anyone who welcomes me also welcomes my Father who sent me. Whoever is the least among you is the greatest."

USING THE NAME OF JESUS

[49] John said to Jesus, "Master, we saw someone using your name to cast out demons, but we told him to stop because he isn't in our group." [50] But Jesus said, "Don't stop him! Anyone who is not against you is for you."

OPPOSITION FROM SAMARITANS

[51] As the time drew near for him to ascend to heaven, Jesus resolutely set out for Jerusalem. [52] He sent messengers ahead to a Samaritan village to prepare for his arrival. [53] But the people of the village did not welcome Jesus because he was on his way to Jerusalem. [54] When James and John saw this, they said to Jesus, "Lord, should we call down fire from heaven to burn them up?" [55] But Jesus turned and rebuked them. [56] So they went on to another village.

THE COST OF FOLLOWING JESUS

[57] As they were walking along, someone said to Jesus, "I will follow you wherever you go." [58] But Jesus replied, "Foxes have dens to live in, and birds have nests, but the Son of Man has no place even to lay his head." [59] He said to another person, "Come, follow me." The man agreed, but he said, "Lord, first let me return home and bury my father." [60] But Jesus told him, "Let the spiritually dead bury their own dead! Your duty is to go and preach about the Kingdom of God." [61] Another said, "Yes, Lord, I will follow you, but first let me say good-bye to my family." [62] But Jesus told him, "Anyone who puts a hand to the plow and then looks back is not fit for the Kingdom of God."

10

JESUS SENDS OUT HIS DISCIPLES

[1] The Lord now chose seventy-two other disciples and sent them ahead in pairs to all the towns and places he planned to visit. [2] These were his instructions to them: "The harvest is great, but the workers are few. So pray to the Lord who is in charge of the harvest; ask him to send more workers into his fields. [3] Now go, and remember that I am sending you out as lambs among wolves. [4] Don't take any money with you, nor a traveler's bag, nor an extra pair of sandals. And don't stop to greet anyone on the road. [5] Whenever you enter someone's home, first say, 'May God's peace be on this house.' [6] If those who live there are peaceful, the blessing will stand; if they are not, the blessing will return to you. [7] Don't move around from home to home. Stay in one place, eating and drinking what they provide. Don't hesitate to accept hospitality, because those who work deserve their pay. [8] If you enter a town and it welcomes you, eat whatever is set before you. [9] Heal the sick, and tell them, 'The Kingdom of God is near you now.' [10] But if a town refuses to welcome you, go out into its streets and say, [11] 'We wipe even the dust of your town from our feet to show that we have abandoned you to your fate. And know this—the Kingdom of God is near!' [12] I assure you, even wicked Sodom will be better off than such a town on judgment day. [13] What sorrow awaits you, Korazin and Bethsaida! For if the miracles I did in you had been done in wicked Tyre and Sidon, their people would have repented of their sins long ago, clothing themselves in burlap and throwing ashes on their heads to show their remorse. [14] Yes, Tyre and Sidon will be better off on judgment day than you. [15] And you people of Capernaum, will you be honored in heaven? No, you will go down to the place of the dead." [16] Then he said to the disciples, "Anyone who accepts your message is also accepting me. And anyone who rejects you is rejecting me. And anyone who rejects me is rejecting God, who sent me."

[17] When the seventy-two disciples returned, they joyfully reported to him, "Lord, even the demons obey us when we use your name!" [18] "Yes," he told them, "I saw Satan fall from heaven like lightning! [19] Look, I have given you authority over all the power of the enemy, and you can walk among snakes and scorpions and crush them. Nothing will injure you. [20] But don't rejoice because evil spirits obey you; rejoice because your names are registered in heaven."

JESUS' PRAYER OF THANKSGIVING

[21] At that same time Jesus was filled with the joy of the Holy Spirit, and he said, "O Father, Lord of heaven and earth, thank you for hiding these things from those who think themselves wise and clever, and for revealing them to the childlike. Yes, Father, it pleased you to do it this way. [22] My Father has entrusted everything to me. No one truly knows the Son except the Father, and no one truly knows the Father except the Son and those to whom the Son chooses to reveal him." [23] Then when they were alone, he turned to the disciples and said, "Blessed are the eyes that see what you have seen. [24] I tell you, many prophets and kings longed to see what you see, but they didn't see it. And they longed to hear what you hear, but they didn't hear it."

THE MOST IMPORTANT COMMANDMENT

[25] One day an expert in religious law stood up to test Jesus by asking him this question: "Teacher, what should I do to inherit eternal life?" [26] Jesus replied, "What does the law of Moses say? How do you read it?" [27] The man answered, "'You must love the LORD your God with all your heart, all your soul, all your strength, and all your mind.' And, 'Love your neighbor as yourself.'" [28] "Right!" Jesus told him. "Do this and you will live!" [29] The man wanted to justify his actions, so he asked Jesus, "And who is my neighbor?"

PARABLE OF THE GOOD SAMARITAN

[30] Jesus replied with a story: "A Jewish man was traveling from Jerusalem down to Jericho, and he was attacked by bandits. They stripped him of his clothes, beat him up, and left him half dead beside the road. [31] By chance a priest came along. But when he saw the man lying there, he crossed to the other side of the road and passed him by. [32] A Temple assistant walked over and looked at him lying there, but he also passed by on the other side. [33] Then a despised Samaritan came along, and when he saw the man, he felt compassion for him. [34] Going over to him, the Samaritan soothed his wounds with olive oil and wine and bandaged them. Then he put the man on his own donkey and took him to an inn, where he took care of him. [35] The next day he handed the innkeeper two silver coins, telling him, 'Take care of this man. If his bill runs higher than this, I'll pay you the next time I'm here.' [36] Now which of these three would you say was a neighbor to the man who was attacked by bandits?" Jesus asked. [37] The man replied, "The one who showed him mercy." Then Jesus said, "Yes, now go and do the same."

JESUS VISITS MARTHA AND MARY

[38] As Jesus and the disciples continued on their way to Jerusalem, they came to a certain village where a woman named Martha welcomed him into her home. [39] Her sister, Mary, sat at the Lord's feet, listening to what he taught. [40] But Martha was distracted by the big dinner she was preparing. She came to Jesus and said, "Lord, doesn't it seem unfair to you that my sister just sits here while I do all the work? Tell her to come and help me." [41] But the Lord said to her, "My dear Martha, you are worried and upset over all these details! [42] There is only one thing worth being concerned about. Mary has discovered it, and it will not be taken away from her."

THE MOST IMPORTANT COMMANDMENT

LUKE 10:25-28

READ

1. Read Luke 10:25-28 slowly (aloud, if it's not intrusive to others).
2. Look at the photos on page 57.
3. Pause.

REFLECT

1. Read the passage again, slowly.
2. What would it be like to love God with the energy displayed in the hands in the upper photo?
3. What would it be like to reach out and help others with the generosity displayed in the action of the hands in the lower photo?
4. Consider why "you will live" if you "do this" (v. 28).
5. What, if anything, do you sense God inviting you to consider?

RESPOND

1. Position your hands as in one of the photos.
2. You might ask God for desire to do this, for empowerment to do this, or for energy to do this.
3. Or you might say with passionate responsiveness: "I want to love the Lord our God with all my heart, all my soul, all my strength, and all my mind! I want to love my neighbor as much as I love myself."

REST

1. Exhale.
2. Rest your hands in your lap, palms facing upward, to receive whatever God wants you to know or be.

11

TEACHING ABOUT PRAYER

[1] Once Jesus was in a certain place praying. As he finished, one of his disciples came to him and said, "Lord, teach us to pray, just as John taught his disciples." [2] Jesus said, "This is how you should pray: "Father, may your name be kept holy. May your Kingdom come soon. [3] Give us each day the food we need, [4] and forgive us our sins, as we forgive those who sin against us. And don't let us yield to temptation." [5] Then, teaching them more about prayer, he used this story: "Suppose you went to a friend's house at midnight, wanting to borrow three loaves of bread. You say to him, [6] 'A friend of mine has just arrived for a visit, and I have nothing for him to eat.' [7] And suppose he calls out from his bedroom, 'Don't bother me. The door is locked for the night, and my family and I are all in bed. I can't help you.' [8] But I tell you this—though he won't do it for friendship's sake, if you keep knocking long enough, he will get up and give you whatever you need because of your shameless persistence. [9] And so I tell you, keep on asking, and you will receive what you ask for. Keep on seeking, and you will find. Keep on knocking, and the door will be opened to you. [10] For everyone who asks, receives. Everyone who seeks, finds. And to everyone who knocks, the door will be opened. [11] You fathers—if your children ask for a fish, do you give them a snake instead? [12] Or if they ask for an egg, do you give them a scorpion? Of course not! [13] So if you sinful people know how to give good gifts to your children, how much more will your heavenly Father give the Holy Spirit to those who ask him."

JESUS AND THE PRINCE OF DEMONS

[14] One day Jesus cast out a demon from a man who couldn't speak, and when the demon was gone, the man began to speak. The crowds were amazed, [15] but some of them said, "No wonder he can cast out demons. He gets his power from Satan, the prince of demons." [16] Others, trying to test Jesus, demanded that he show them a miraculous sign from heaven to prove his authority. [17] He knew their thoughts, so he said, "Any kingdom divided by civil war is doomed. A family splintered by feuding will fall apart. [18] You say I am empowered by Satan. But if Satan is divided and fighting against himself, how can his kingdom survive? [19] And if I am empowered by Satan, what about your own exorcists? They cast out demons, too, so they will condemn you for what you have said. [20] But if I am casting out demons by the power of God, then the Kingdom of God has arrived among you. [21] For when a strong man is fully armed and guards his palace, his possessions are safe— [22] until someone even stronger attacks and overpowers him, strips him of his weapons, and carries off his belongings. [23] Anyone who isn't with me opposes me, and anyone who isn't working with me is actually working against me. [24] When an evil spirit leaves a person, it goes into the desert, searching for rest. But when it finds none, it says, 'I will return to the person I came from.' [25] So it returns and finds that its former home is all swept and in order. [26] Then the spirit finds seven other spirits more evil than itself, and they all enter the person and live there. And so that person is worse off than before." [27] As he was speaking, a woman in the crowd called out, "God bless your mother—the womb from which you came, and the breasts that nursed you!" [28] Jesus replied, "But even more blessed are all who hear the word of God and put it into practice."

THE SIGN OF JONAH

[29] As the crowd pressed in on Jesus, he said, "This evil generation keeps asking me to show them a miraculous sign. But the only sign I will give them is the sign of Jonah. [30] What happened to him was a sign to the people of Nineveh that God had sent him. What happens to the Son of Man will be a sign to these people that he was sent by God. [31] The queen of Sheba will stand up against this generation on judgment day and condemn it, for she came from a distant land to hear the wisdom of Solomon. Now someone greater than Solomon is here—but you refuse to listen. [32] The people of Nineveh will also stand up against this generation on judgment day and condemn it, for they repented of their sins at the preaching of Jonah. Now someone greater than Jonah is here—but you refuse to repent.

RECEIVING THE LIGHT

[33] "No one lights a lamp and then hides it or puts it under a basket. Instead, a lamp is placed on a stand, where its light can be seen by all who enter the house. [34] Your eye is like a lamp that provides light for your body. When your eye is healthy, your whole body is filled with light. But when it is unhealthy, your body is filled with darkness. [35] Make sure that the light you think you have is not actually darkness. [36] If you are filled with light, with no dark corners, then your whole life will be radiant, as though a floodlight were filling you with light."

JESUS CRITICIZES THE RELIGIOUS LEADERS

[37] As Jesus was speaking, one of the Pharisees invited him home for a meal. So he went in and took his place at the table. [38] His host was amazed to see that he sat down to eat without first performing the hand-washing

ceremony required by Jewish custom. ³⁹ Then the Lord said to him, "You Pharisees are so careful to clean the outside of the cup and the dish, but inside you are filthy—full of greed and wickedness! ⁴⁰ Fools! Didn't God make the inside as well as the outside? ⁴¹ So clean the inside by giving gifts to the poor, and you will be clean all over. ⁴² What sorrow awaits you Pharisees! For you are careful to tithe even the tiniest income from your herb gardens, but you ignore justice and the love of God. You should tithe, yes, but do not neglect the more important things. ⁴³ What sorrow awaits you Pharisees! For you love to sit in the seats of honor in the synagogues and receive respectful greetings as you walk in the marketplaces. ⁴⁴ Yes, what sorrow awaits you! For you are like hidden graves in a field. People walk over them without knowing the corruption they are stepping on." ⁴⁵ "Teacher," said an expert in religious law, "you have insulted us, too, in what you just said." ⁴⁶ "Yes," said Jesus, "what sorrow also awaits you experts in religious law! For you crush people with unbearable religious demands, and you never lift a finger to ease the burden. ⁴⁷ What sorrow awaits you! For you build monuments for the prophets your own ancestors killed long ago. ⁴⁸ But in fact, you stand as witnesses who agree with what your ancestors did. They killed the prophets, and you join in their crime by building the monuments! ⁴⁹ This is what God in his wisdom said about you: 'I will send prophets and apostles to them, but they will kill some and persecute the others.' ⁵⁰ As a result, this generation will be held responsible for the murder of all God's prophets from the creation of the world— ⁵¹ from the murder of Abel to the murder of Zechariah, who was killed between the altar and the sanctuary. Yes, it will certainly be charged against this generation. ⁵² What sorrow awaits you experts in religious law! For you remove the key to knowledge from the people. You don't enter the Kingdom yourselves, and you prevent others from entering." ⁵³ As Jesus was leaving, the teachers of religious law and the Pharisees became hostile and tried to provoke him with many questions. ⁵⁴ They wanted to trap him into saying something they could use against him.

JESUS CRITICIZES THE RELIGIOUS LEADERS

LUKE 11:37-52

READ

1. Read Luke 11:37-52 slowly.
2. Look at the photo on page 63.
3. Pause.

REFLECT

1. Read the passage again, aloud and slowly. Beginning in verse 40, read Jesus' words in an intense way. You may express that intensity in a strong whisper or more loudly. Keep in mind how Jesus grieved—even wept—over Israel's leadership (Luke 19:41).
2. Notice what word or phrase resonates with you. Why do you think that is?
3. In the photo, notice that the normal arrangement of chairs has become confused and jumbled. In Jesus' eyes, the Pharisees had done this to God's Kingdom. In the Pharisees' eyes, Jesus was turning the Kingdom of God upside down.
4. Is there a situation for which your heart aches because of the sorrow involved in jumbled views of God, of what God wants, or of how God works?

RESPOND

1. Consider who or what God is inviting you to pray for now.
2. You may wish to grieve with God over the sorrow that comes from not entering the Kingdom and preventing others from doing so (v. 52).

REST

1. Exhale.
2. Rest in the thought that the Kingdom of God is held carefully by God, and God will do what is needed to help people enter it.

12

A WARNING AGAINST HYPOCRISY

[1] Meanwhile, the crowds grew until thousands were milling about and stepping on each other. Jesus turned first to his disciples and warned them, "Beware of the yeast of the Pharisees—their hypocrisy. [2] The time is coming when everything that is covered up will be revealed, and all that is secret will be made known to all. [3] Whatever you have said in the dark will be heard in the light, and what you have whispered behind closed doors will be shouted from the housetops for all to hear! [4] Dear friends, don't be afraid of those who want to kill your body; they cannot do any more to you after that. [5] But I'll tell you whom to fear. Fear God, who has the power to kill you and then throw you into hell. Yes, he's the one to fear. [6] What is the price of five sparrows—two copper coins? Yet God does not forget a single one of them. [7] And the very hairs on your head are all numbered. So don't be afraid; you are more valuable to God than a whole flock of sparrows. [8] I tell you the truth, everyone who acknowledges me publicly here on earth, the Son of Man will also acknowledge in the presence of God's angels. [9] But anyone who denies me here on earth will be denied before God's angels. [10] Anyone who speaks against the Son of Man can be forgiven, but anyone who blasphemes the Holy Spirit will not be forgiven. [11] And when you are brought to trial in the synagogues and before rulers and authorities, don't worry about how to defend yourself or what to say, [12] for the Holy Spirit will teach you at that time what needs to be said."

PARABLE OF THE RICH FOOL

[13] Then someone called from the crowd, "Teacher, please tell my brother to divide our father's estate with me." [14] Jesus replied, "Friend, who made me a judge over you to decide such things as that?" [15] Then he said, "Beware! Guard against every kind of greed. Life is not measured by how much you own." [16] Then he told them a story: "A rich man had a fertile farm that produced fine crops. [17] He said to himself, 'What should I do? I don't have room for all my crops.' [18] Then he said, 'I know! I'll tear down my barns and build bigger ones. Then I'll have room enough to store all my wheat and other goods. [19] And I'll sit back and say to myself, "My friend, you have enough stored away for years to come. Now take it easy! Eat, drink, and be merry!"' [20] But God said to him, 'You fool! You will die this very night. Then who will get everything you worked for?' [21] Yes, a person is a fool to store up earthly wealth but not have a rich relationship with God."

TEACHING ABOUT MONEY AND POSSESSIONS

[22] Then, turning to his disciples, Jesus said, "That is why I tell you not to worry about everyday life—whether you have enough food to eat or enough clothes to wear. [23] For life is more than food, and your body more than clothing. [24] Look at the ravens. They don't plant or harvest or store food in barns, for God feeds them. And you are far more valuable to him than any birds! [25] Can all your worries add a single moment to your life? [26] And if worry can't accomplish a little thing like that, what's the use of worrying over bigger things? [27] Look at the lilies and how they grow. They don't work or make their clothing, yet Solomon in all his glory was not dressed as beautifully as they are. [28] And if God cares so wonderfully for flowers that are here today and thrown into the fire tomorrow, he will certainly care for you. Why do you have so little faith? [29] And don't be concerned about what to eat and what to drink. Don't worry about such things. [30] These things dominate the thoughts of unbelievers all over the world, but your Father already knows your needs. [31] Seek the Kingdom of God above all else, and he will give you everything you need. [32] So don't be afraid, little flock. For it gives your Father great happiness to give you the Kingdom. [33] Sell your possessions and give to those in need. This will store up treasure for you in heaven! And the purses of heaven never get old or develop holes. Your treasure will be safe; no thief can steal it and no moth can destroy it. [34] Wherever your treasure is, there the desires of your heart will also be.

BE READY FOR THE LORD'S COMING

[35] "Be dressed for service and keep your lamps burning, [36] as though you were waiting for your master to return from the wedding feast. Then you will be ready to open the door and let him in the moment he arrives and knocks. [37] The servants who are ready and waiting for his return will be rewarded. I tell you the truth, he himself will seat them, put on an apron, and serve them as they sit and eat! [38] He may come in the middle of the night or just before dawn. But whenever he comes, he will reward the servants who are ready. [39] Understand this: If a homeowner knew exactly when a burglar was coming, he would not permit his house to be broken into. [40] You also must be ready all the time, for the Son of Man will come when least expected." [41] Peter asked, "Lord, is that illustration just for us or for everyone?" [42] And the Lord replied, "A faithful, sensible servant is one to whom the master can give the responsibility of managing his other household servants and feeding them. [43] If the master returns and finds that the servant has done a good job, there will be a reward. [44] I tell you the truth, the master will put that servant in charge of all he owns. [45] But what if the servant thinks, 'My master won't be back for a while,' and he begins beating the other servants, partying, and getting drunk? [46] The master will return unannounced and unexpected, and he will cut the servant in pieces and banish him with the unfaithful. [47] And a servant who knows what the master wants, but isn't prepared and doesn't carry out those instructions, will be severely punished. [48] But someone who does not know, and then does something wrong, will be punished only lightly. When someone has been given much, much will be required in return; and when someone has been entrusted with much, even more will be required.

JESUS CAUSES DIVISION

[49] "I have come to set the world on fire, and I wish it were already burning! [50] I have a terrible baptism of suffering ahead of me, and I am under a heavy burden until it is accomplished. [51] Do you think I have come to bring peace to the earth? No, I have come to divide people against each other! [52] From now on families will be split apart, three in favor of me, and two against— or two in favor and three against. [53] 'Father will be divided against son and son against father; mother against daughter and daughter against mother; and mother-in-law against daughter-in-law and daughter-in-law against mother-in-law.'" [54] Then Jesus turned to the crowd and said, "When you see clouds beginning to form in the west, you say, 'Here comes a shower.' And you are right. [55] When the south wind blows, you say, 'Today will be a scorcher.' And it is. [56] You fools! You know how to interpret the weather signs of the earth and sky, but you don't know how to interpret the present times. [57] Why can't you decide for yourselves what is right? [58] When you are on the way to court with your accuser, try to settle the matter before you get there. Otherwise, your accuser may drag you before the judge, who will hand you over to an officer, who will throw you into prison. [59] And if that happens, you won't be free again until you have paid the very last penny."

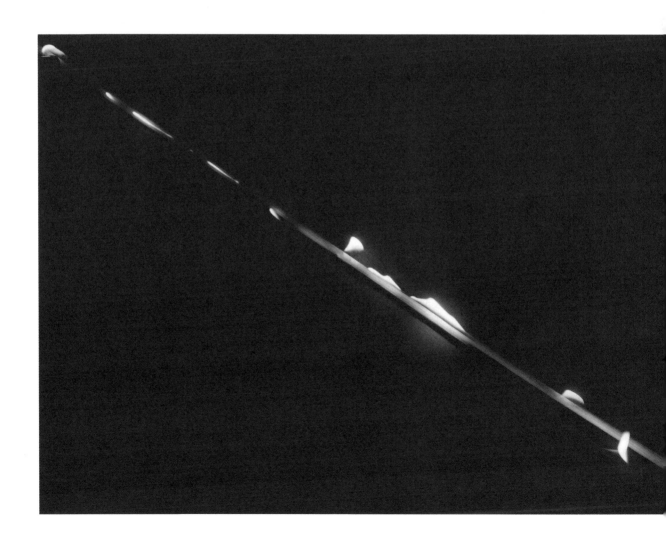

13

A CALL TO REPENTANCE

[1] About this time Jesus was informed that Pilate had murdered some people from Galilee as they were offering sacrifices at the Temple. [2] "Do you think those Galileans were worse sinners than all the other people from Galilee?" Jesus asked. "Is that why they suffered? [3] Not at all! And you will perish, too, unless you repent of your sins and turn to God. [4] And what about the eighteen people who died when the tower in Siloam fell on them? Were they the worst sinners in Jerusalem? [5] No, and I tell you again that unless you repent, you will perish, too."

PARABLE OF THE BARREN FIG TREE

[6] Then Jesus told this story: "A man planted a fig tree in his garden and came again and again to see if there was any fruit on it, but he was always disappointed. [7] Finally, he said to his gardener, 'I've waited three years, and there hasn't been a single fig! Cut it down. It's just taking up space in the garden.' [8] The gardener answered, 'Sir, give it one more chance. Leave it another year, and I'll give it special attention and plenty of fertilizer. [9] If we get figs next year, fine. If not, then you can cut it down.'"

JESUS HEALS ON THE SABBATH

[10] One Sabbath day as Jesus was teaching in a synagogue, [11] he saw a woman who had been crippled by an evil spirit. She had been bent double for eighteen years and was unable to stand up straight. [12] When Jesus saw her, he called her over and said, "Dear woman, you are healed of your sickness!" [13] Then he touched her, and instantly she could stand straight. How she praised God! [14] But the leader in charge of the synagogue was indignant that Jesus had healed her on the Sabbath day. "There are six days of the week for working," he said to the crowd. "Come on those days to be healed, not on the Sabbath." [15] But the Lord replied, "You hypocrites! Each of you works on the Sabbath day! Don't you untie your ox or your donkey from its stall on the Sabbath and lead it out for water? [16] This dear woman, a daughter of Abraham, has been held in bondage by Satan for eighteen years. Isn't it right that she be released, even on the Sabbath?" [17] This shamed his enemies, but all the people rejoiced at the wonderful things he did.

PARABLE OF THE MUSTARD SEED

[18] Then Jesus said, "What is the Kingdom of God like? How can I illustrate it? [19] It is like a tiny mustard seed that a man planted in a garden; it grows and becomes a tree, and the birds make nests in its branches."

PARABLE OF THE YEAST

[20] He also asked, "What else is the Kingdom of God like? [21] It is like the yeast a woman used in making bread. Even though she put only a little yeast in three measures of flour, it permeated every part of the dough."

JESUS HEALS ON THE SABBATH

LUKE 13:10-17

READ

1. Read Luke 13:10-17 slowly (aloud, if it's not in-trusive to others).
2. Look at the photo on page 72.
3. Pause.

REFLECT

1. Read the passage again, slowly.
2. Stand up. Bend over at the waist and walk slowly about five feet. Notice what you can see and not see.
3. Next, stand up as straight as the woman in the photo. How does it feel to finally stand up straight? Consider how appropriate this stance is for the Sabbath.

RESPOND

1. Read the passage one more time. This time notice if you find yourself in the passage—perhaps as the woman, the leader of the synagogue, those sitting in the synagogue who rejoiced, the disciples who came in with Jesus, or a "fly on the wall" watching it all happen.
2. From the place or person you have found yourself in, say (aloud, if possible) to God what you most desire to say or to see happen in your life.

REST

1. Sit down and exhale.
2. If you wish, take time to worship Jesus—God in the flesh—who saw this woman's agony and helped her at a cost to himself.

THE NARROW DOOR

[22] Jesus went through the towns and villages, teaching as he went, always pressing on toward Jerusalem. [23] Someone asked him, "Lord, will only a few be saved?" He replied, [24] "Work hard to enter the narrow door to God's Kingdom, for many will try to enter but will fail. [25] When the master of the house has locked the door, it will be too late. You will stand outside knocking and pleading, 'Lord, open the door for us!' But he will reply, 'I don't know you or where you come from.' [26] Then you will say, 'But we ate and drank with you, and you taught in our streets.' [27] And he will reply, 'I tell you, I don't know you or where you come from. Get away from me, all you who do evil.' [28] There will be weeping and gnashing of teeth, for you will see Abraham, Isaac, Jacob, and all the prophets in the Kingdom of God, but you will be thrown out. [29] And people will come from all over the world—from east and west, north and south—to take their places in the Kingdom of God. [30] And note this: Some who seem least important now will be the greatest then, and some who are the greatest now will be least important then."

JESUS GRIEVES OVER JERUSALEM

[31] At that time some Pharisees said to him, "Get away from here if you want to live! Herod Antipas wants to kill you!" [32] Jesus replied, "Go tell that fox that I will keep on casting out demons and healing people today and tomorrow; and the third day I will accomplish my purpose. [33] Yes, today, tomorrow, and the next day I must proceed on my way. For it wouldn't do for a prophet of God to be killed except in Jerusalem! [34] O Jerusalem, Jerusalem, the city that kills the prophets and stones God's messengers! How often I have wanted to gather your children together as a hen protects her chicks beneath her wings, but you wouldn't let me. [35] And now, look, your house is abandoned. And you will never see me again until you say, 'Blessings on the one who comes in the name of the Lord!'"

14

JESUS HEALS ON THE SABBATH

[1] One Sabbath day Jesus went to eat dinner in the home of a leader of the Pharisees, and the people were watching him closely. [2] There was a man there whose arms and legs were swollen. [3] Jesus asked the Pharisees and experts in religious law, "Is it permitted in the law to heal people on the Sabbath day, or not?" [4] When they refused to answer, Jesus touched the sick man and healed him and sent him away. [5] Then he turned to them and said, "Which of you doesn't work on the Sabbath? If your son or your cow falls into a pit, don't you rush to get him out?" [6] Again they could not answer.

JESUS TEACHES ABOUT HUMILITY

[7] When Jesus noticed that all who had come to the dinner were trying to sit in the seats of honor near the head of the table, he gave them this advice: [8] "When you are invited to a wedding feast, don't sit in the seat of honor. What if someone who is more distinguished than you has also been invited? [9] The host will come and say, 'Give this person your seat.' Then you will be embarrassed, and you will have to take whatever seat is left at the foot of the table! [10] Instead, take the lowest place at the foot of the table. Then when your host sees you, he will come and say, 'Friend, we have a better place for you!' Then you will be honored in front of all the other guests. [11] For those who exalt themselves will be humbled, and those who humble themselves will be exalted." [12] Then he turned to his host. "When you put on a luncheon or a banquet," he said, "don't invite your friends, brothers, relatives, and rich neighbors. For they will invite you back, and that will be your only reward. [13] Instead, invite the poor, the crippled, the lame, and the blind. [14] Then at the resurrection of the righteous, God will reward you for inviting those who could not repay you."

PARABLE OF THE GREAT FEAST

[15] Hearing this, a man sitting at the table with Jesus exclaimed, "What a blessing it will be to attend a banquet in the Kingdom of God!" [16] Jesus replied with this story: "A man prepared a great feast and sent out many invitations. [17] When the banquet was ready, he sent his servant to tell the guests, 'Come, the banquet is ready.' [18] But they all began making excuses. One said, 'I have just bought a field and must inspect it. Please excuse me.' [19] Another said, 'I have just bought five pairs of oxen, and I want to try them out. Please excuse me.' [20] Another said, 'I just got married, so I can't come.' [21] The servant returned and told his master what they had said. His master was furious and said, 'Go quickly into the streets and alleys of the town and invite the poor, the crippled, the blind, and the lame.' [22] After the servant had done this, he reported, 'There is still room for more.' [23] So his master said, 'Go out into the country lanes and behind the hedges and urge anyone you find to come, so that the house will be full. [24] For none of those I first invited will get even the smallest taste of my banquet.'"

PARABLE OF THE GREAT FEAST

LUKE 14:15-24

READ

1. Read Luke 14:15-24 slowly (aloud, if it's not intrusive to others).
2. Look at the photos on page 78.
3. Pause.

REFLECT

1. Read verses 15-17 again, slowly, and look at the photo of the sumptuous banquet food on the right. Consider how it felt to prepare such a banquet and gaze at all the lavish food. Imagine the fashionable, upscale chairs that would surround a table such as this.
2. Read verses 18-24 again, slowly, and look at the haphazard stacking of the mediocre chair and stool by the fence in the alley. Imagine what sort of persons would ordinarily be sitting there and how they might respond to an invitation to a banquet.

3. What, if anything, do you sense God inviting you to consider?

RESPOND

1. How do you respond to Jesus' picturing God the Father (or perhaps the entire Trinity) as a party-planning banquet host? What does this invite you to say to God at this moment—about the banquet, about the ones who didn't come, or about the ones who did come?
2. What do you find yourself desiring at this moment that you may want to talk to God about?

REST

1. Exhale.
2. Spend a few moments being glad that God is involved in joyous activities and inviting others into them "so that the house will be full" (v. 23).

THE COST OF BEING A DISCIPLE

[25] A large crowd was following Jesus. He turned around and said to them,
[26] "If you want to be my disciple, you must, by comparison, hate everyone
else—your father and mother, wife and children, brothers and sisters—yes,
even your own life. Otherwise, you cannot be my disciple. [27] And if you
do not carry your own cross and follow me, you cannot be my disciple.
[28] But don't begin until you count the cost. For who would begin construc-
tion of a building without first calculating the cost to see if there is enough
money to finish it? [29] Otherwise, you might complete only the foundation
before running out of money, and then everyone would laugh at you.
[30] They would say, 'There's the person who started that building and
couldn't afford to finish it!' [31] Or what king would go to war against another
king without first sitting down with his counselors to discuss whether his
army of 10,000 could defeat the 20,000 soldiers marching against him?
[32] And if he can't, he will send a delegation to discuss terms of peace while
the enemy is still far away. [33] So you cannot become my disciple without
giving up everything you own. [34] Salt is good for seasoning. But if it loses
its flavor, how do you make it salty again? [35] Flavorless salt is good neither
for the soil nor for the manure pile. It is thrown away. Anyone with ears
to hear should listen and understand!"

15

PARABLE OF THE LOST SHEEP

[1] Tax collectors and other notorious sinners often came to listen to Jesus teach. [2] This made the Pharisees and teachers of religious law complain that he was associating with such sinful people—even eating with them! [3] So Jesus told them this story: [4] "If a man has a hundred sheep and one of them gets lost, what will he do? Won't he leave the ninety-nine others in the wilderness and go to search for the one that is lost until he finds it? [5] And when he has found it, he will joyfully carry it home on his shoulders. [6] When he arrives, he will call together his friends and neighbors, saying, 'Rejoice with me because I have found my lost sheep.' [7] In the same way, there is more joy in heaven over one lost sinner who repents and returns to God than over ninety-nine others who are righteous and haven't strayed away!

PARABLE OF THE LOST COIN

[8] "Or suppose a woman has ten silver coins and loses one. Won't she light a lamp and sweep the entire house and search carefully until she finds it? [9] And when she finds it, she will call in her friends and neighbors and say, 'Rejoice with me because I have found my lost coin.' [10] In the same way, there is joy in the presence of God's angels when even one sinner repents."

PARABLE OF THE LOST SON

[11] To illustrate the point further, Jesus told them this story: "A man had two sons. [12] The younger son told his father, 'I want my share of your estate now before you die.' So his father agreed to divide his wealth between his sons. [13] A few days later this younger son packed all his belongings and moved to a distant land, and there he wasted all his money in wild living. [14] About the time his money ran out, a great famine swept over the land, and he began to starve. [15] He persuaded a local farmer to hire him, and the man sent him into his fields to feed the pigs. [16] The young man became so hungry that even the pods he was feeding the pigs looked good to him. But no one gave him anything. [17] When he finally came to his senses, he said to himself, 'At home even the hired servants have food enough to spare, and here I am dying of hunger! [18] I will go home to my father and say, "Father, I have sinned against both heaven and you, [19] and I am no longer worthy of being called your son. Please take me on as a hired servant."' [20] So he returned home to his father. And while he was still a long way off, his father saw him coming. Filled with love and compassion, he ran to his son, embraced him, and kissed him. [21] His son said to him, 'Father, I have sinned against both heaven and you, and I am no longer worthy of being called your son.' [22] But his father said to the servants, 'Quick! Bring the finest robe in the house and put it on him. Get a ring for his finger and sandals for his feet. [23] And kill the calf we have been fattening. We must celebrate with a feast, [24] for this son of mine was dead and has now returned to life. He was lost, but now he is found.' So the party began. [25] Meanwhile, the older son was in the fields working. When he returned home, he heard music and dancing in the house, [26] and he asked one of the servants what was going on. [27] 'Your brother is back,' he was told, 'and your father has killed the fattened calf. We are celebrating because of his safe return.' [28] The older brother was angry and wouldn't go in. His father came out and begged him, [29] but he replied, 'All these years I've slaved for you and never once refused to do a single thing you told me to. And in all that time you never gave me even one young goat for a feast with my friends. [30] Yet when this son of yours comes back after squandering your money on prostitutes, you celebrate by killing the fattened calf!' [31] His father said to him, 'Look, dear son, you have always stayed by me, and everything I have is yours. [32] We had to celebrate this happy day. For your brother was dead and has come back to life! He was lost, but now he is found!'"

PARABLE OF THE LOST SON

LUKE 15:11-24

READ

1. Read Luke 15:11-24 slowly (aloud, if it's not intrusive to others).
2. Pause.

REFLECT

1. Read the passage again, slowly.
2. Notice what word or phrase or moment in the story stands out to you. If you perhaps found yourself in the passage, if only as a bystander looking on, consider what that is like for you. How do you respond to these events?

RESPOND

1. The younger son lived out a dramatic journey. Talk to God about where you are in your journey.

2. Ask God whatever you wish to know about the next step of your journey. What do you need to move forward?

REST

1. Read verse 24 again and look at the photo of the balloons on page 84. How might the younger son have felt to be included in such a party?
2. Exhale.
3. Remember with affection and gratefulness the "balloon moments" of your journey.

A BEGGING FATHER

LUKE 15:25-32

READ

1. Read Luke 15:25-32 slowly (aloud, if it's not intrusive to others).
2. Look at the photo on page 85.
3. Pause.

REFLECT

1. Read the passage again, slowly.
2. Notice what moments or words or phrases catch your attention.
3. What emotions would the older son have been feeling? How would it have felt to stay outside and look in through the window at the party inside?
4. What emotions would the father have been feeling as he begged his older son to come in? As he said, "Everything I have is yours"?

5. What invitations or appeals, if any, do you sense God setting before you?

RESPOND

1. What does this passage and the story Jesus told make you want to say to God?
2. Is there something you wish to understand? To grow in? To be grateful for?

REST

1. Exhale.
2. Jesus left this story unfinished. Consider what it would have been like if the older son got up and went into the party.

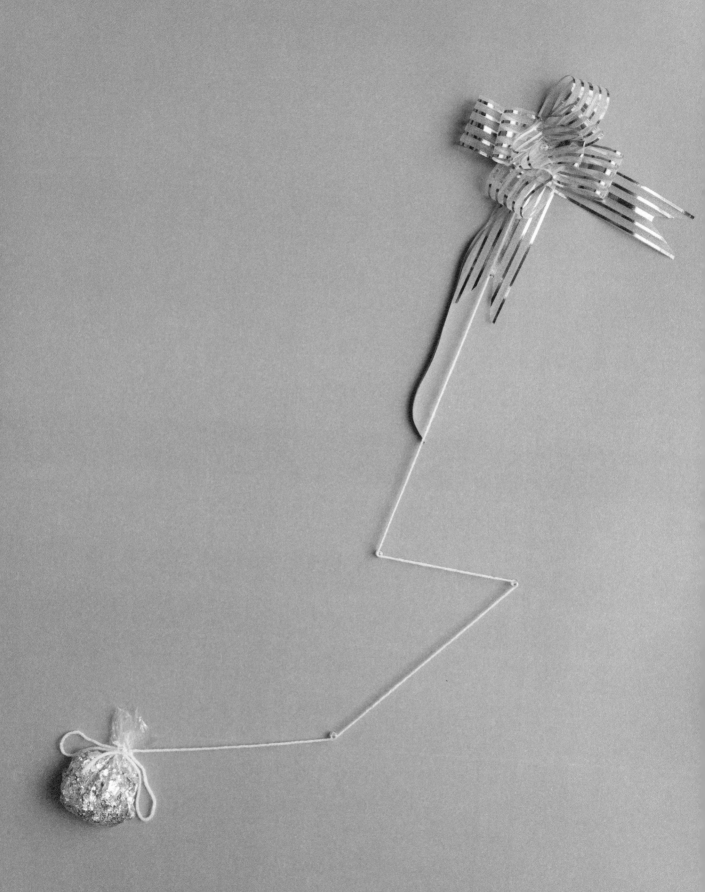

16

PARABLE OF THE SHREWD MANAGER

[1] Jesus told this story to his disciples: "There was a certain rich man who had a manager handling his affairs. One day a report came that the manager was wasting his employer's money. [2] So the employer called him in and said, 'What's this I hear about you? Get your report in order, because you are going to be fired.' [3] The manager thought to himself, 'Now what? My boss has fired me. I don't have the strength to dig ditches, and I'm too proud to beg. [4] Ah, I know how to ensure that I'll have plenty of friends who will give me a home when I am fired.' [5] So he invited each person who owed money to his employer to come and discuss the situation. He asked the first one, 'How much do you owe him?' [6] The man replied, 'I owe him 800 gallons of olive oil.' So the manager told him, 'Take the bill and quickly change it to 400 gallons.' [7] 'And how much do you owe my employer?' he asked the next man. 'I owe him 1,000 bushels of wheat,' was the reply. 'Here,' the manager said, 'take the bill and change it to 800 bushels.' [8] The rich man had to admire the dishonest rascal for being so shrewd. And it is true that the children of this world are more shrewd in dealing with the world around them than are the children of the light. [9] Here's the lesson: Use your worldly resources to benefit others and make friends. Then, when your possessions are gone, they will welcome you to an eternal home. [10] If you are faithful in little things, you will be faithful in large ones. But if you are dishonest in little things, you won't be honest with greater responsibilities. [11] And if you are untrustworthy about worldly wealth, who will trust you with the true riches of heaven? [12] And if you are not faithful with other people's things, why should you be trusted with things of your own? [13] No one can serve two masters. For you will hate one and love the other; you will be devoted to one and despise the other. You cannot serve God and be enslaved to money." [14] The Pharisees, who dearly loved their money, heard all this and scoffed at him. [15] Then he said to them, "You like to appear righteous in public, but God knows your hearts. What this world honors is detestable in the sight of God. [16] Until John the Baptist, the law of Moses and the messages of the prophets were your guides. But now the Good News of the Kingdom of God is preached, and everyone is eager to get in. [17] But that doesn't mean that the law has lost its force. It is easier for heaven and earth to disappear than for the smallest point of God's law to be overturned. [18] For example, a man who divorces his wife and marries someone else commits adultery. And anyone who marries a woman divorced from her husband commits adultery."

PARABLE OF THE RICH MAN AND LAZARUS

¹⁹ Jesus said, "There was a certain rich man who was splendidly clothed in purple and fine linen and who lived each day in luxury. ²⁰ At his gate lay a poor man named Lazarus who was covered with sores. ²¹ As Lazarus lay there longing for scraps from the rich man's table, the dogs would come and lick his open sores. ²² Finally, the poor man died and was carried by the angels to sit beside Abraham at the heavenly banquet. The rich man also died and was buried, ²³ and he went to the place of the dead. There, in torment, he saw Abraham in the far distance with Lazarus at his side. ²⁴ The rich man shouted, 'Father Abraham, have some pity! Send Lazarus over here to dip the tip of his finger in water and cool my tongue. I am in anguish in these flames.' ²⁵ But Abraham said to him, 'Son, remember that during your lifetime you had everything you

wanted, and Lazarus had nothing. So now he is here being comforted, and you are in anguish. [26] And besides, there is a great chasm separating us. No one can cross over to you from here, and no one can cross over to us from there.' [27] Then the rich man said, 'Please, Father Abraham, at least send him to my father's home. [28] For I have five brothers, and I want him to warn them so they don't end up in this place of torment.' [29] But Abraham said, 'Moses and the prophets have warned them. Your brothers can read what they wrote.' [30] The rich man replied, 'No, Father Abraham! But if someone is sent to them from the dead, then they will repent of their sins and turn to God.' [31] But Abraham said, 'If they won't listen to Moses and the prophets, they won't be persuaded even if someone rises from the dead.'"

17

TEACHINGS ABOUT FORGIVENESS AND FAITH

[1] One day Jesus said to his disciples, "There will always be temptations to sin, but what sorrow awaits the person who does the tempting! [2] It would be better to be thrown into the sea with a millstone hung around your neck than to cause one of these little ones to fall into sin. [3] So watch yourselves! If another believer sins, rebuke that person; then if there is repentance, forgive. [4] Even if that person wrongs you seven times a day and each time turns again and asks forgiveness, you must forgive." [5] The apostles said to the Lord, "Show us how to increase our faith." [6] The Lord answered, "If you had faith even as small as a mustard seed, you could say to this mulberry tree, 'May you be uprooted and be planted in the sea,' and it would obey you! [7] When a servant comes in from plowing or taking care of sheep, does his master say, 'Come in and eat with me'? [8] No, he says, 'Prepare my meal, put on your apron, and serve me while I eat. Then you can eat later.' [9] And does the master thank the servant for doing what he was told to do? Of course not. [10] In the same way, when you obey me you should say, 'We are unworthy servants who have simply done our duty.'"

TEN HEALED OF LEPROSY

[11] As Jesus continued on toward Jerusalem, he reached the border between Galilee and Samaria. [12] As he entered a village there, ten men with leprosy stood at a distance, [13] crying out, "Jesus, Master, have mercy on us!" [14] He looked at them and said, "Go show yourselves to the priests." And as they went, they were cleansed of their leprosy. [15] One of them, when he saw that he was healed, came back to Jesus, shouting, "Praise God!" [16] He fell to the ground at Jesus' feet, thanking him for what he had done. This man was a Samaritan. [17] Jesus asked, "Didn't I heal ten men? Where are the other nine? [18] Has no one returned to give glory to God except this foreigner?" [19] And Jesus said to the man, "Stand up and go. Your faith has healed you."

THE COMING OF THE KINGDOM

[20] One day the Pharisees asked Jesus, "When will the Kingdom of God come?" Jesus replied, "The Kingdom of God can't be detected by visible signs. [21] You won't be able to say, 'Here it is!' or 'It's over there!' For the Kingdom of God is already among you." [22] Then he said to his disciples, "The time is coming when you will long to see the day when the Son of Man returns, but you won't see it. [23] People will tell you, 'Look, there is the Son of Man,' or 'Here he is,' but don't go out and follow them. [24] For as the lightning flashes and lights up the sky from one end to the other, so it will be on the day when the Son of Man comes. [25] But first the Son of Man must suffer terribly and be rejected by this generation. [26] When the Son of Man returns, it will be like it was in Noah's day. [27] In those days, the people enjoyed banquets and parties and weddings right up to the time Noah entered his boat and the flood came and destroyed them all. [28] And the world will be as it was in the days of Lot. People went about their daily business—eating and drinking, buying and selling, farming and building— [29] until the morning Lot left Sodom. Then fire and burning sulfur rained down from heaven and destroyed them all. [30] Yes, it will be 'business as usual' right up to the day when the Son of Man is revealed. [31] On that day a person out on the deck of a roof must not go down into the house to pack. A person out in the field must not return home. [32] Remember what happened to Lot's wife! [33] If you cling to your life, you will lose it, and if you let your life go, you will save it. [34] That night two people will be asleep in one bed; one will be taken, the other left. [35] Two women will be grinding flour together at the mill; one will be taken, the other left." [37] "Where will this happen, Lord?" the disciples asked. Jesus replied, "Just as the gathering of vultures shows there is a carcass nearby, so these signs indicate that the end is near."

18

PARABLE OF THE PERSISTENT WIDOW

[1] One day Jesus told his disciples a story to show that they should always pray and never give up. [2] "There was a judge in a certain city," he said, "who neither feared God nor cared about people. [3] A widow of that city came to him repeatedly, saying, 'Give me justice in this dispute with my enemy.' [4] The judge ignored her for a while, but finally he said to himself, 'I don't fear God or care about people, [5] but this woman is driving me crazy. I'm going to see that she gets justice, because she is wearing me out with her constant requests!'" [6] Then the Lord said, "Learn a lesson from this unjust judge. [7] Even he rendered a just decision in the end. So don't you think God will surely give justice to his chosen people who cry out to him day and night? Will he keep putting them off? [8] I tell you, he will grant justice to them quickly! But when the Son of Man returns, how many will he find on the earth who have faith?"

PARABLE OF THE PHARISEE AND TAX COLLECTOR

[9] Then Jesus told this story to some who had great confidence in their own righteousness and scorned everyone else: [10] "Two men went to the Temple to pray. One was a Pharisee, and the other was a despised tax collector. [11] The Pharisee stood by himself and prayed this prayer: 'I thank you, God, that I am not like other people—cheaters, sinners, adulterers. I'm certainly not like that tax collector! [12] I fast twice a week, and I give you a tenth of my income.' [13] But the tax collector stood at a distance and dared not even lift his eyes to heaven as he prayed. Instead, he beat his chest in sorrow, saying, 'O God, be merciful to me, for I am a sinner.' [14] I tell you, this sinner, not the Pharisee, returned home justified before God. For those who exalt themselves will be humbled, and those who humble themselves will be exalted."

JESUS BLESSES THE CHILDREN

[15] One day some parents brought their little children to Jesus so he could touch and bless them. But when the disciples saw this, they scolded the parents for bothering him. [16] Then Jesus called for the children and said to the disciples, "Let the children come to me. Don't stop them! For the Kingdom of God belongs to those who are like these children. [17] I tell you the truth, anyone who doesn't receive the Kingdom of God like a child will never enter it."

THE RICH MAN

[18] Once a religious leader asked Jesus this question: "Good Teacher, what should I do to inherit eternal life?" [19] "Why do you call me good?" Jesus asked him. "Only God is truly good. [20] But to answer your question, you know the commandments: 'You must not commit adultery. You must not murder. You must not steal. You must not testify falsely. Honor your father and mother.'" [21] The man replied, "I've obeyed all these commandments since I was young." [22] When Jesus heard his answer, he said, "There is still one thing you haven't done. Sell all your possessions and give the money to the poor, and you will have treasure in heaven. Then come, follow me." [23] But when the man heard this he became very sad, for he was very rich. [24] When Jesus saw this, he said, "How hard it is for the rich to enter the Kingdom of God! [25] In fact, it is easier for a camel to go through the eye of a needle than for a rich person to enter the Kingdom of God!" [26] Those who heard this said, "Then who in the world can be saved?" [27] He replied, "What is impossible for people is possible with God." [28] Peter said, "We've left our homes to follow you." [29] "Yes," Jesus replied, "and I assure you that everyone who has given up house or wife or brothers or parents or children, for the sake of the Kingdom of God, [30] will be repaid many times over in this life, and will have eternal life in the world to come."

JESUS AGAIN PREDICTS HIS DEATH

[31] Taking the twelve disciples aside, Jesus said, "Listen, we're going up to Jerusalem, where all the predictions of the prophets concerning the Son of Man will come true. [32] He will be handed over to the Romans, and he will be mocked, treated shamefully, and spit upon. [33] They will flog him with a whip and kill him, but on the third day he will rise again." [34] But they didn't understand any of this. The significance of his words was hidden from them, and they failed to grasp what he was talking about.

JESUS HEALS A BLIND BEGGAR

[35] As Jesus approached Jericho, a blind beggar was sitting beside the road. [36] When he heard the noise of a crowd going past, he asked what was happening. [37] They told him that Jesus the Nazarene was going by. [38] So he began shouting, "Jesus, Son of David, have mercy on me!" [39] "Be quiet!" the people in front yelled at him. But he only shouted louder, "Son of David, have mercy on me!" [40] When Jesus heard him, he stopped and ordered that the man be brought to him. As the man came near, Jesus asked him, [41] "What do you want me to do for you?" "Lord," he said, "I want to see!" [42] And Jesus said, "All right, receive your sight! Your faith has healed you." [43] Instantly the man could see, and he followed Jesus, praising God. And all who saw it praised God, too.

19

JESUS AND ZACCHAEUS

¹ Jesus entered Jericho and made his way through the town. ² There was a man there named Zacchaeus. He was the chief tax collector in the region, and he had become very rich. ³ He tried to get a look at Jesus, but he was too short to see over the crowd. ⁴ So he ran ahead and climbed a sycamore-fig tree beside the road, for Jesus was going to pass that way. ⁵ When Jesus came by, he looked up at Zacchaeus and called him by name. "Zacchaeus!" he said. "Quick, come down! I must be a guest in your home today." ⁶ Zacchaeus quickly climbed down and took Jesus to his house in great excitement and joy. ⁷ But the people were displeased. "He has gone to be the guest of a notorious sinner," they grumbled. ⁸ Meanwhile, Zacchaeus stood before the Lord and said, "I will give half my wealth to the poor, Lord, and if I have cheated people on their taxes, I will give them back four times as much!" ⁹ Jesus responded, "Salvation has come to this home today, for this man has shown himself to be a true son of Abraham. ¹⁰ For the Son of Man came to seek and save those who are lost."

PARABLE OF THE TEN SERVANTS

¹¹ The crowd was listening to everything Jesus said. And because he was nearing Jerusalem, he told them a story to correct the impression that the Kingdom of God would begin right away. ¹² He said, "A nobleman was called away to a distant empire to be crowned king and then return. ¹³ Before he left, he called together ten of his servants and divided among them ten pounds of silver, saying, 'Invest this for me while I am gone.' ¹⁴ But his people hated him and sent a delegation after him to say, 'We do not want him to be our king.' ¹⁵ After he was crowned king, he returned and called in the servants to whom he had given the money. He wanted to find out what their profits were. ¹⁶ The first servant reported, 'Master, I invested your money and made ten times the original amount!' ¹⁷ 'Well done!' the king exclaimed. 'You are a good servant. You have been faithful with the little I entrusted to you, so you will be governor of ten cities as your reward.' ¹⁸ The next servant reported, 'Master, I invested your money and made five times the original amount.' ¹⁹ 'Well done!' the king said. 'You will be governor over five cities.' ²⁰ But the third servant brought back only the original amount of money and said, 'Master, I hid your money and kept it safe. ²¹ I was afraid because you are a hard man to deal with, taking what isn't yours and harvesting crops you didn't plant.' ²² 'You wicked servant!' the king roared. 'Your own words condemn you. If you knew that I'm a hard man who takes what isn't mine and harvests crops I didn't plant, ²³ why didn't you deposit my money in the bank? At least I could have gotten some interest on it.' ²⁴ Then, turning to the others standing nearby, the king ordered, 'Take the money from this servant, and give it to the one who has ten pounds.' ²⁵ 'But, master,' they said, 'he already has ten pounds!' ²⁶ 'Yes,' the king replied, 'and to those who use well what they are given, even more will be given. But from those who do nothing, even what little they have will be taken away. ²⁷ And as for these enemies of mine who didn't want me to be their king—bring them in and execute them right here in front of me.'"

JESUS AND ZACCHAEUS

LUKE 19:1-10

READ

1. Read Luke 19:1-10 slowly.
2. Look at the photo on page 100. Notice that the top of the tree, where a notorious tax collector could safely hide, is hidden from your view.
3. Pause.

REFLECT

1. Read the passage again, slowly.
2. Imagine yourself as an onlooker in this Jericho crowd of people. How do you respond to this powerful "chief" official coming down out of hiding to talk with Jesus?
3. Jesus initially intended to only make "his way through the town" but changed his mind when he noticed someone who others thought would be the last person he should associate with. How do you respond to this upside-down Kingdom of God? Are you uncomfortable? Surprised? Intrigued? Amused? Delighted?

4. What, if anything, do you sense God inviting you to consider about Jesus?

RESPOND

1. Ask God to bring to mind someone you know and love or possibly dislike. Talk to God about how this person might be persuaded to move out of a place of hiding (emotionally, socially, physically).
2. Consider asking God who or what the ladder might be in such a situation.

REST

1. Exhale.
2. Rest in the extravagant generosity of the "Son of Man [who] came to seek and save those who are lost" in some way (v. 10).

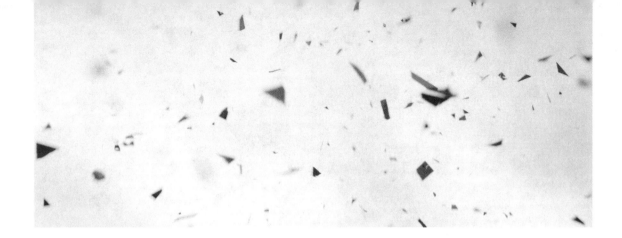

JESUS' TRIUMPHANT ENTRY

[28] After telling this story, Jesus went on toward Jerusalem, walking ahead of his disciples. [29] As he came to the towns of Bethphage and Bethany on the Mount of Olives, he sent two disciples ahead. [30] "Go into that village over there," he told them. "As you enter it, you will see a young donkey tied there that no one has ever ridden. Untie it and bring it here. [31] If anyone asks, 'Why are you untying that colt?' just say, 'The Lord needs it.'" [32] So they went and found the colt, just as Jesus had said. [33] And sure enough, as they were untying it, the owners asked them, "Why are you untying that colt?" [34] And the disciples simply replied, "The Lord needs it." [35] So they brought the colt to Jesus and threw their garments over it for him to ride on. [36] As he rode along, the crowds spread out their garments on the road ahead of him. [37] When he reached the place where the road started down the Mount of Olives, all of his followers began to shout and sing as they walked along, praising God for all the wonderful miracles they had seen. [38] "Blessings on the King who comes in the name of the Lord! Peace in heaven, and glory in highest heaven!" [39] But some of the Pharisees among the crowd said, "Teacher, rebuke your followers for saying things like that!" [40] He replied, "If they kept quiet, the stones along the road would burst into cheers!"

JESUS WEEPS OVER JERUSALEM

[41] But as he came closer to Jerusalem and saw the city ahead, he began to weep. [42] "How I wish today that you of all people would understand the way to peace. But now it is too late, and peace is hidden from your eyes. [43] Before long your enemies will build ramparts against your walls and encircle you and close in on you from every side. [44] They will crush you into the ground, and your children with you. Your enemies will not leave a single stone in place, because you did not recognize it when God visited you."

JESUS CLEARS THE TEMPLE

[45] Then Jesus entered the Temple and began to drive out the people selling animals for sacrifices. [46] He said to them, "The Scriptures declare, 'My Temple will be a house of prayer,' but you have turned it into a den of thieves." [47] After that, he taught daily in the Temple, but the leading priests, the teachers of religious law, and the other leaders of the people began planning how to kill him. [48] But they could think of nothing, because all the people hung on every word he said.

JESUS CLEARS THE TEMPLE

LUKE 19:45-48

READ

1. Read Luke 19:45-48 very slowly (aloud, if it's not intrusive to others).
2. Look at the photo on page 104.
3. Pause.

REFLECT

1. Read the passage again, slowly.
2. Look at the photo again. Why is there so much darkness?
3. Imagine yourself in this scene, watching the true Master of the temple enter and bring light. How are you touched by the flame of Jesus' desire that the temple be a house of prayer?
4. What, if anything, do you sense God inviting you to embrace or let go of?

RESPOND

1. Place your hand on the photo just over the shaft of light.
2. Thank God that Jesus brings truth and light into dark places—within you, with those who know something of God, with those throughout the world who do not.

REST

1. Exhale.
2. If you're willing, hold the idea that Jesus brings striking, surprising shafts of light to our lives every day.

20

THE AUTHORITY OF JESUS CHALLENGED

[1] One day as Jesus was teaching the people and preaching the Good News in the Temple, the leading priests, the teachers of religious law, and the elders came up to him. [2] They demanded, "By what authority are you doing all these things? Who gave you the right?" [3] "Let me ask you a question first," he replied. [4] "Did John's authority to baptize come from heaven, or was it merely human?" [5] They talked it over among themselves. "If we say it was from heaven, he will ask why we didn't believe John. [6] But if we say it was merely human, the people will stone us because they are convinced John was a prophet." [7] So they finally replied that they didn't know. [8] And Jesus responded, "Then I won't tell you by what authority I do these things."

PARABLE OF THE EVIL FARMERS

[9] Now Jesus turned to the people again and told them this story: "A man planted a vineyard, leased it to tenant farmers, and moved to another country to live for several years. [10] At the time of the grape harvest, he sent one of his servants to collect his share of the crop. But the farmers attacked the servant, beat him up, and sent him back empty-handed. [11] So the owner sent another servant, but they also insulted him, beat him up, and sent him away empty-handed. [12] A third man was sent, and they wounded him and chased him away. [13] 'What will I do?' the owner asked himself. 'I know! I'll send my cherished son. Surely they will respect him.' [14] But when the tenant farmers saw his son, they said to each other, 'Here comes the heir to this estate. Let's kill him and get the estate for ourselves!' [15] So they dragged him out of the vineyard and murdered him. What do you suppose the owner of the vineyard will do to them?" Jesus asked. [16] "I'll tell you—he will come and kill those farmers and lease the vineyard to others." "How terrible that such a thing should ever happen," his listeners protested. [17] Jesus looked at them and said, "Then what does this Scripture mean? 'The stone that the builders rejected has now become the cornerstone.' [18] Everyone who stumbles over that stone will be broken to pieces, and it will crush anyone it falls on." [19] The teachers of religious law and the leading priests wanted to arrest Jesus immediately because they realized he was telling the story against them—they were the wicked farmers. But they were afraid of the people's reaction.

TAXES FOR CAESAR

[20] Watching for their opportunity, the leaders sent spies pretending to be honest men. They tried to get Jesus to say something that could be reported to the Roman governor so he would arrest Jesus. [21] "Teacher," they said, "we know that you speak and teach what is right and are not influenced by what others think. You teach the way of God truthfully. [22] Now tell us—is it right for us to pay taxes to Caesar or not?" [23] He saw through their trickery and said, [24] "Show me a Roman coin. Whose picture and title are stamped on it?" "Caesar's," they replied. [25] "Well then," he said, "give to Caesar what belongs to Caesar, and give to God what belongs to God." [26] So they failed to trap him by what he said in front of the people. Instead, they were amazed by his answer, and they became silent.

DISCUSSION ABOUT RESURRECTION

[27] Then Jesus was approached by some Sadducees—religious leaders who say there is no resurrection from the dead. [28] They posed this question: "Teacher, Moses gave us a law that if a man dies, leaving a wife but no children, his brother should marry the widow and have a child who will carry on the brother's name. [29] Well, suppose there were seven brothers. The oldest one married and then died without children. [30] So the second brother married the widow, but he also died. [31] Then the third brother married her. This continued with all seven of them, who died without children. [32] Finally, the woman also died. [33] So tell us, whose wife will she be in the resurrection? For all seven were married to her!" [34] Jesus replied, "Marriage is for people here on earth. [35] But in the age to come, those worthy of being raised from the dead will neither marry nor be given in marriage. [36] And they will never die again. In this respect they will be like angels. They are children of God and children of the resurrection. [37] But now, as to whether the dead will be raised—even Moses proved this when he wrote about the burning bush. Long after Abraham, Isaac, and Jacob had died, he referred to the Lord as 'the God of Abraham, the God of Isaac, and the God of Jacob.' [38] So he is the God of the living, not the dead, for they are all alive to him." [39] "Well said, Teacher!" remarked some of the teachers of religious law who were standing there. [40] And then no one dared to ask him any more questions.

WHOSE SON IS THE MESSIAH?

[41] Then Jesus presented them with a question. "Why is it," he asked, "that the Messiah is said to be the son of David? [42] For David himself wrote in the book of Psalms: 'The LORD said to my Lord, Sit in the place of honor at my right hand [43] until I humble your enemies, making them a footstool under your feet.' [44] Since David called the Messiah 'Lord,' how can the Messiah be his son?" [45] Then, with the crowds listening, he turned to his disciples and said, [46] "Beware of these teachers of religious law! For they like to parade around in flowing robes and love to receive respectful greetings as they walk in the marketplaces. And how they love the seats of honor in the synagogues and the head table at banquets. [47] Yet they shamelessly cheat widows out of their property and then pretend to be pious by making long prayers in public. Because of this, they will be severely punished."

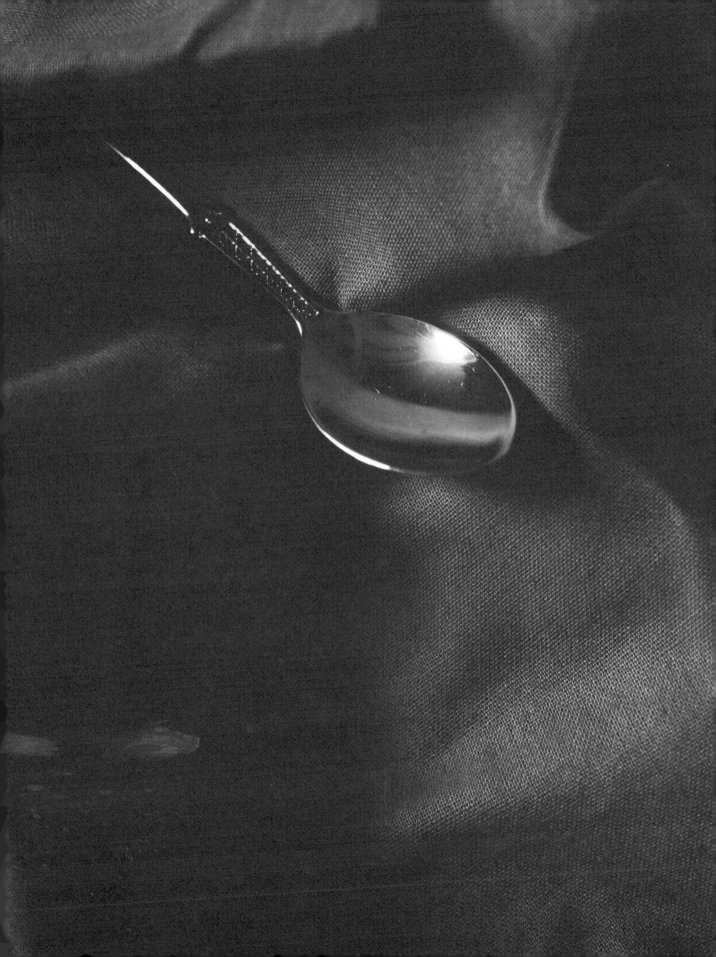

21

THE WIDOW'S OFFERING

[1] While Jesus was in the Temple, he watched the rich people dropping their gifts in the collection box. [2] Then a poor widow came by and dropped in two small coins. [3] "I tell you the truth," Jesus said, "this poor widow has given more than all the rest of them. [4] For they have given a tiny part of their surplus, but she, poor as she is, has given everything she has."

JESUS SPEAKS ABOUT THE FUTURE

[5] Some of his disciples began talking about the majestic stonework of the Temple and the memorial decorations on the walls. But Jesus said, [6] "The time is coming when all these things will be completely demolished. Not one stone will be left on top of another!" [7] "Teacher," they asked, "when will all this happen? What sign will show us that these things are about to take place?" [8] He replied, "Don't let anyone mislead you, for many will come in my name, claiming, 'I am the Messiah,' and saying, 'The time has come!' But don't believe them. [9] And when you hear of wars and insurrections, don't panic. Yes, these things must take place first, but the end won't follow immediately." [10] Then he added, "Nation will go to war against nation, and kingdom against kingdom. [11] There will be great earthquakes, and there will be famines and plagues in many lands, and there will be terrifying things and great miraculous signs from heaven. [12] But before all this occurs, there will be a time of great persecution. You will be dragged into synagogues and prisons, and you will stand trial before kings and governors because you are my followers. [13] But this will be your opportunity to tell them about me. [14] So don't worry in advance about how to answer the charges against you, [15] for I will give you the right words and such wisdom that none of your opponents will be able to reply or refute you! [16] Even those closest to you—your parents, brothers, relatives, and friends—will betray you. They will even kill some of you. [17] And everyone will hate you because you are my followers. [18] But not a hair of your head will perish! [19] By standing firm, you will win your souls. [20] And when you see Jerusalem surrounded by armies, then you will know that the time of its destruction has arrived. [21] Then those in Judea must flee to the hills. Those in Jerusalem must get out, and those out in the country should not return to the city. [22] For those will be days of God's vengeance, and the prophetic words of the Scriptures will be fulfilled. [23] How terrible it will be for pregnant women and for nursing mothers in those days. For there will be disaster in the land and great anger against this people. [24] They will be killed by the sword or sent away as captives to all the nations of the world. And Jerusalem will be trampled down by the Gentiles until the period of the Gentiles comes to an end. [25] And there will be strange signs in the sun, moon, and stars. And here on earth the nations will be in turmoil, perplexed by the roaring seas and strange tides. [26] People will be terrified at what they see coming upon the earth, for the powers in the heavens will be shaken. [27] Then everyone will see the Son of Man coming on a cloud with power and great glory. [28] So when all these things begin to happen, stand and look up, for your salvation is near!" [29] Then he gave them this illustration: "Notice the fig tree, or any other tree. [30] When the leaves come out, you know without being told that summer is near. [31] In the same way, when you see all these things taking place, you can know that the Kingdom of God is near. [32] I tell you the truth, this generation will not pass from the scene until all these things have taken place. [33] Heaven and earth will disappear, but my words will never disappear. [34] Watch out! Don't let your hearts be dulled by carousing and drunkenness, and by the worries of this life. Don't let that day catch you unaware, [35] like a trap. For that day will come upon everyone living on the earth. [36] Keep alert at all times. And pray that you might be strong enough to escape these coming horrors and stand before the Son of Man." [37] Every day Jesus went to the Temple to teach, and each evening he returned to spend the night on the Mount of Olives. [38] The crowds gathered at the Temple early each morning to hear him.

22

JUDAS AGREES TO BETRAY JESUS

[1] The Festival of Unleavened Bread, which is also called Passover, was approaching. [2] The leading priests and teachers of religious law were plotting how to kill Jesus, but they were afraid of the people's reaction. [3] Then Satan entered into Judas Iscariot, who was one of the twelve disciples, [4] and he went to the leading priests and captains of the Temple guard to discuss the best way to betray Jesus to them. [5] They were delighted, and they promised to give him money. [6] So he agreed and began looking for an opportunity to betray Jesus so they could arrest him when the crowds weren't around.

THE LAST SUPPER

[7] Now the Festival of Unleavened Bread arrived, when the Passover lamb is sacrificed. [8] Jesus sent Peter and John ahead and said, "Go and prepare the Passover meal, so we can eat it together." [9] "Where do you want us to prepare it?" they asked him. [10] He replied, "As soon as you enter Jerusalem, a man carrying a pitcher of water will meet you. Follow him. At the house he enters, [11] say to the owner, 'The Teacher asks: Where is the guest room where I can eat the Passover meal with my disciples?' [12] He will take you upstairs to a large room that is already set up. That is where you should prepare our meal." [13] They went off to the city and found everything just as Jesus had said, and they prepared the Passover meal there. [14] When the time came, Jesus and the apostles sat down together at the table. [15] Jesus said, "I have been very eager to eat this Passover meal with you before my suffering begins. [16] For I tell you now that I won't eat this meal again until its meaning is fulfilled in the Kingdom of God." [17] Then he took a cup of wine and gave thanks to God for it. Then he said, "Take this and share it among yourselves. [18] For I will not drink wine again until the Kingdom of God has come." [19] He took some bread and gave thanks to God for it. Then he broke it in pieces and gave it to the disciples, saying, "This is my body, which is given for you. Do this in remembrance of me." [20] After supper he took another cup of wine and said, "This cup is the new covenant between God and his people—an agreement confirmed with my blood, which is poured out as a sacrifice for you. [21] But here at this table, sitting among us as a friend, is the man who will betray me. [22] For it has been determined that the Son of Man must die. But what sorrow awaits the one who betrays him." [23] The disciples began to ask each other which of them would ever do such a thing. [24] Then they began to argue among themselves about who would be the greatest among them. [25] Jesus told them, "In this world the kings and great men lord it over their people, yet they are called 'friends of the people.' [26] But among you it will be different. Those who are the greatest among you should take the lowest rank, and the leader should be like a servant. [27] Who is more important, the one who sits at the table or the one who serves? The one who sits at the table, of course. But not here! For I am among you as one who serves. [28] You have stayed with me in my time of trial. [29] And just as my Father has granted me a Kingdom, I now grant you the right [30] to eat and drink at my table in my Kingdom. And you will sit on thrones, judging the twelve tribes of Israel.

JESUS PREDICTS PETER'S DENIAL

31 "Simon, Simon, Satan has asked to sift each of you like wheat. 32 But I have pleaded in prayer for you, Simon, that your faith should not fail. So when you have repented and turned to me again, strengthen your brothers." 33 Peter said, "Lord, I am ready to go to prison with you, and even to die with you." 34 But Jesus said, "Peter, let me tell you something. Before the rooster crows tomorrow morning, you will deny three times that you even know me." 35 Then Jesus asked them, "When I sent you out to preach the Good News and you did not have money, a traveler's bag, or an extra pair of sandals, did you need anything?" "No," they replied. 36 "But now," he said, "take your money and a traveler's bag. And if you don't have a sword, sell your cloak and buy one! 37 For the time has come for this prophecy about me to be fulfilled: 'He was counted among the rebels.' Yes, everything written about me by the prophets will come true." 38 "Look, Lord," they replied, "we have two swords among us." "That's enough," he said.

JESUS PRAYS ON THE MOUNT OF OLIVES

39 Then, accompanied by the disciples, Jesus left the upstairs room and went as usual to the Mount of Olives. 40 There he told them, "Pray that you will not give in to temptation." 41 He walked away, about a stone's throw, and knelt down and prayed, 42 "Father, if you are willing, please take this cup of suffering away from me. Yet I want your will to be done, not mine." 43 Then an angel from heaven appeared and strengthened him. 44 He prayed more fervently, and he was in such agony of spirit that his sweat fell to the ground like great drops of blood. 45 At last he stood up again and returned to the disciples, only to find them asleep, exhausted from grief. 46 "Why are you sleeping?" he asked them. "Get up and pray, so that you will not give in to temptation."

JESUS IS BETRAYED AND ARRESTED

47 But even as Jesus said this, a crowd approached, led by Judas, one of the twelve disciples. Judas walked over to Jesus to greet him with a kiss. 48 But Jesus said, "Judas, would you betray the Son of Man with a kiss?" 49 When the other disciples saw what was about to happen, they exclaimed, "Lord, should we fight? We brought the swords!" 50 And one of them struck at the high priest's slave, slashing off his right ear. 51 But Jesus said, "No more of this." And he touched the man's ear and healed him. 52 Then Jesus spoke to the leading priests, the captains of the Temple guard, and the elders who had come for him. "Am I some dangerous revolutionary," he asked, "that you come with swords and clubs to arrest me? 53 Why didn't you arrest me in the Temple? I was there every day. But this is your moment, the time when the power of darkness reigns."

PETER DENIES JESUS

54 So they arrested him and led him to the high priest's home. And Peter followed at a distance. 55 The guards lit a fire in the middle of the courtyard and sat around it, and Peter joined them there. 56 A servant girl noticed him in the firelight and began staring at him. Finally she said, "This man was one of Jesus' followers!" 57 But Peter denied it. "Woman," he said, "I don't even know him!" 58 After a while someone else looked at him and said, "You must be one of them!" "No, man, I'm not!" Peter retorted. 59 About an hour later someone else insisted, "This must be one of them, because he is a Galilean, too." 60 But Peter said, "Man, I don't know what you are talking about." And immediately, while he was still speaking, the rooster crowed. 61 At that moment the Lord turned and looked at Peter. Suddenly, the Lord's words flashed through Peter's mind: "Before the rooster crows tomorrow morning, you will deny three times that you even know me." 62 And Peter left the courtyard, weeping bitterly. 63 The guards in charge of Jesus began mocking and beating him. 64 They blindfolded him and said, "Prophesy to us! Who hit you that time?" 65 And they hurled all sorts of terrible insults at him.

JESUS BEFORE THE COUNCIL

[66] At daybreak all the elders of the people assembled, including the leading priests and the teachers of religious law. Jesus was led before this high council, [67] and they said, "Tell us, are you the Messiah?" But he replied, "If I tell you, you won't believe me. [68] And if I ask you a question, you won't answer. [69] But from now on the Son of Man will be seated in the place of power at God's right hand." [70] They all shouted, "So, are you claiming to be the Son of God?" And he replied, "You say that I am." [71] "Why do we need other witnesses?" they said. "We ourselves heard him say it."

23

JESUS' TRIAL BEFORE PILATE

¹ Then the entire council took Jesus to Pilate, the Roman governor. ² They began to state their case: "This man has been leading our people astray by telling them not to pay their taxes to the Roman government and by claiming he is the Messiah, a king." ³ So Pilate asked him, "Are you the king of the Jews?" Jesus replied, "You have said it." ⁴ Pilate turned to the leading priests and to the crowd and said, "I find nothing wrong with this man!" ⁵ Then they became insistent. "But he is causing riots by his teaching wherever he goes—all over Judea, from Galilee to Jerusalem!" ⁶ "Oh, is he a Galilean?" Pilate asked. ⁷ When they said that he was, Pilate sent him to Herod Antipas, because Galilee was under Herod's jurisdiction, and Herod happened to be in Jerusalem at the time. ⁸ Herod was delighted at the opportunity to see Jesus, because he had heard about him and had been hoping for a long time to see him perform a miracle. ⁹ He asked Jesus question after question, but Jesus refused to answer. ¹⁰ Meanwhile, the leading priests and the teachers of religious law stood there shouting their accusations. ¹¹ Then Herod and his soldiers began mocking and ridiculing Jesus. Finally, they put a royal robe on him and sent him back to Pilate. ¹² (Herod and Pilate, who had been enemies before, became friends that day.) ¹³ Then Pilate called together the leading priests and other religious leaders, along with the people, ¹⁴ and he announced his verdict. "You brought this man to me, accusing him of leading a revolt. I have examined him thoroughly on this point in your presence and find him innocent. ¹⁵ Herod came to the same conclusion and sent him back to us. Nothing this man has done calls for the death penalty. ¹⁶ So I will have him flogged, and then I will release him."

¹⁸ Then a mighty roar rose from the crowd, and with one voice they shouted, "Kill him, and release Barabbas to us!" ¹⁹ (Barabbas was in prison for taking part in an insurrection in Jerusalem against the government, and for murder.) ²⁰ Pilate argued with them, because he wanted to release Jesus. ²¹ But they kept shouting, "Crucify him! Crucify him!" ²² For the third time he demanded, "Why? What crime has he committed? I have found no reason to sentence him to death. So I will have him flogged, and then I will release him." ²³ But the mob shouted louder and louder, demanding that Jesus be crucified, and their voices prevailed. ²⁴ So Pilate sentenced Jesus to die as they demanded. ²⁵ As they had requested, he released Barabbas, the man in prison for insurrection and murder. But he turned Jesus over to them to do as they wished.

THE CRUCIFIXION

²⁶ As they led Jesus away, a man named Simon, who was from Cyrene, happened to be coming in from the countryside. The soldiers seized him and put the cross on him and made him carry it behind Jesus. ²⁷ A large crowd trailed behind, including many grief-stricken women. ²⁸ But Jesus turned and said to them, "Daughters of Jerusalem, don't weep for me, but weep for yourselves and for your children. ²⁹ For the days are coming when they will say, 'Fortunate indeed are the women who are childless, the wombs that have not borne a child

and the breasts that have never nursed.' [30] People will beg the mountains, 'Fall on us,' and plead with the hills, 'Bury us.' [31] For if these things are done when the tree is green, what will happen when it is dry?" [32] Two others, both criminals, were led out to be executed with him. [33] When they came to a place called The Skull, they nailed him to the cross. And the criminals were also crucified—one on his right and one on his left. [34] Jesus said, "Father, forgive them, for they don't know what they are doing." And the soldiers gambled for his clothes by throwing dice. [35] The crowd watched and the leaders scoffed. "He saved others," they said, "let him save himself if he is really God's Messiah, the Chosen One." [36] The soldiers mocked him, too, by offering him a drink of sour wine. [37] They called out to him, "If you are the King of the Jews, save yourself!" [38] A sign was fastened above him with these words: "This is the King of the Jews." [39] One of the criminals hanging beside him scoffed, "So you're the Messiah, are you? Prove it by saving yourself—and us, too, while you're at it!" [40] But the other criminal protested, "Don't you fear God even when you have been sentenced to die? [41] We deserve to die for our crimes, but this man hasn't done anything wrong." [42] Then he said, "Jesus, remember me when you come into your Kingdom." [43] And Jesus replied, "I assure you, today you will be with me in paradise."

THE DEATH OF JESUS

[44] By this time it was about noon, and darkness fell across the whole land until three o'clock. [45] The light from the sun was gone. And suddenly, the curtain in the sanctuary of the Temple was torn down the middle. [46] Then Jesus shouted, "Father, I entrust my spirit into your hands!" And with those words he breathed his last. [47] When the Roman officer overseeing the execution saw what had happened, he worshiped God and said, "Surely this man was innocent." [48] And when all the crowd that came to see the crucifixion saw what had happened, they went home in deep sorrow. [49] But Jesus' friends, including the women who had followed him from Galilee, stood at a distance watching.

THE BURIAL OF JESUS

[50] Now there was a good and righteous man named Joseph. He was a member of the Jewish high council, [51] but he had not agreed with the decision and actions of the other religious leaders. He was from the town of Arimathea in Judea, and he was waiting for the Kingdom of God to come. [52] He went to Pilate and asked for Jesus' body. [53] Then he took the body down from the cross and wrapped it in a long sheet of linen cloth and laid it in a new tomb that had been carved out of rock. [54] This was done late on Friday afternoon, the day of preparation, as the Sabbath was about to begin. [55] As his body was taken away, the women from Galilee followed and saw the tomb where his body was placed. [56] Then they went home and prepared spices and ointments to anoint his body. But by the time they were finished the Sabbath had begun, so they rested as required by the law.

24

THE RESURRECTION

[1] But very early on Sunday morning the women went to the tomb, taking the spices they had prepared. [2] They found that the stone had been rolled away from the entrance. [3] So they went in, but they didn't find the body of the Lord Jesus. [4] As they stood there puzzled, two men suddenly appeared to them, clothed in dazzling robes. [5] The women were terrified and bowed with their faces to the ground. Then the men asked, "Why are you looking among the dead for someone who is alive? [6] He isn't here! He is risen from the dead! Remember what he told you back in Galilee, [7] that the Son of Man must be betrayed into the hands of sinful men and be crucified, and that he would rise again on the third day." [8] Then they remembered that he had said this. [9] So they rushed back from the tomb to tell his eleven disciples—and everyone else—what had happened. [10] It was Mary Magdalene, Joanna, Mary the mother of James, and several other women who told the apostles what had happened. [11] But the story sounded like nonsense to the men, so they didn't believe it. [12] However, Peter jumped up and ran to the tomb to look. Stooping, he peered in and saw the empty linen wrappings; then he went home again, wondering what had happened.

JESUS BEFORE THE COUNCIL, AND THE RESURRECTION

LUKE 22:66-71; 24:1-8

READ

1. Read Luke 22:66-71 and 24:1-8 slowly (aloud, if it's not intrusive to others).
2. Look at the photos on pages 116-19.
3. Pause.

REFLECT

1. Read Luke 22:66-71 again, slowly.
2. Notice how the intensity builds in the passage as Jesus and the religious leaders interact. Notice also how the intensity builds from the smaller photo (p. 116) to the full-page photo (p. 117) to the double-page photo (pp. 118-19). Stay with the double-page photo to absorb the immensity of the consequences brought about by the council. What words or feelings come to you?
3. Pause and exhale.
4. Read Luke 24:1-8 again and look at the photo on page 122. How do you respond to the way the grave clothes appear to be effortlessly tossed around the tree to indicate that the person once dead is alive?
5. What, if anything, do you sense God inviting you to consider about Jesus? About how God works?

RESPOND

1. Talk to God about what impresses you most about Jesus.
2. What was Jesus willing to do? Or what was Jesus capable of?

REST

1. Exhale.
2. If you're willing, pick up the book and hold it close in front of you open to page 122. This illustration of immense power is designed to be part of a person's life in the Kingdom of God here and now.

THE WALK TO EMMAUS

[13] That same day two of Jesus' followers were walking to the village of Emmaus, seven miles from Jerusalem. [14] As they walked along they were talking about everything that had happened. [15] As they talked and discussed these things, Jesus himself suddenly came and began walking with them. [16] But God kept them from recognizing him. [17] He asked them, "What are you discussing so intently as you walk along?" They stopped short, sadness written across their faces. [18] Then one of them, Cleopas, replied, "You must be the only person in Jerusalem who hasn't heard about all the things that have happened there the last few days." [19] "What things?" Jesus asked. "The things that happened to Jesus, the man from Nazareth," they said. "He was a prophet who did powerful miracles, and he was a mighty teacher in the eyes of God and all the people. [20] But our leading priests and other religious leaders handed him over to be condemned to death, and they crucified him. [21] We had hoped he was the Messiah who had come to rescue Israel. This all happened three days ago. [22] Then some women from our group of his followers were at his tomb early this morning, and they came back with an amazing report. [23] They said his body was missing, and they had seen angels who told them Jesus is alive! [24] Some of our men ran out to see, and sure enough, his body was gone, just as the women had said." [25] Then Jesus said to them, "You foolish people! You find it so hard to believe all that the prophets wrote in the Scriptures. [26] Wasn't it clearly predicted that the Messiah would have to suffer all these things before entering his glory?" [27] Then Jesus took them through the writings of Moses and all the prophets, explaining from all the Scriptures the things concerning himself. [28] By this time they were nearing Emmaus and the end of their journey. Jesus acted as if he were going on, [29] but they begged him, "Stay the night with us, since it is getting late." So he went home with them. [30] As they sat down to eat, he took the bread and blessed it. Then he broke it and gave it to them. [31] Suddenly, their eyes were opened, and they recognized him. And at that moment he disappeared! [32] They said to each other, "Didn't our hearts burn within us as he talked with us on the road and explained the Scriptures to us?" [33] And within the hour they were on their way back to Jerusalem. There they found the eleven disciples and the others who had gathered with them, [34] who said, "The Lord has really risen! He appeared to Peter."

JESUS APPEARS TO THE DISCIPLES

35 Then the two from Emmaus told their story of how Jesus had appeared to them as they were walking along the road, and how they had recognized him as he was breaking the bread. 36 And just as they were telling about it, Jesus himself was suddenly standing there among them. "Peace be with you," he said. 37 But the whole group was startled and frightened, thinking they were seeing a ghost! 38 "Why are you frightened?" he asked. "Why are your hearts filled with doubt? 39 Look at my hands. Look at my feet. You can see that it's really me. Touch me and make sure that I am not a ghost, because ghosts don't have bodies, as you see that I do." 40 As he spoke, he showed them his hands and his feet. 41 Still they stood there in disbelief, filled with joy and wonder. Then he asked them, "Do you have anything here to eat?" 42 They gave him a piece of broiled fish, 43 and he ate it as they watched. 44 Then he said, "When I was with you before, I told you that everything written about me in the law of Moses and the prophets and in the Psalms must be fulfilled." 45 Then he opened their minds to understand the Scriptures. 46 And he said, "Yes, it was written long ago that the Messiah would suffer and die and rise from the dead on the third day. 47 It was also written that this message would be proclaimed in the authority of his name to all the nations, beginning in Jerusalem: 'There is forgiveness of sins for all who repent.' 48 You are witnesses of all these things. 49 And now I will send the Holy Spirit, just as my Father promised. But stay here in the city until the Holy Spirit comes and fills you with power from heaven."

THE ASCENSION

50 Then Jesus led them to Bethany, and lifting his hands to heaven, he blessed them. 51 While he was blessing them, he left them and was taken up to heaven. 52 So they worshiped him and then returned to Jerusalem filled with great joy. 53 And they spent all of their time in the Temple, praising God.

LIST OF GUIDED MEDITATIONS

CONTINUE THE CONVERSATION

www.alabasterco.com